Celtic

Robert Van de Weyer is a
responsibility for two rural parishes, and an inner city
ecumenical congregation; and he is the founder of the
modern Little Gidding Community. He is the author of
numerous books, including two on Celtic spirituality,
Celtic Fire (DLT) and *Celtic Parables* (SPCK); and he is
also a frequent broadcaster. He is married to Sarah,
and they have two grown-up sons.

BY THE SAME AUTHOR

*Celtic Fire: An Anthology of Celtic
Christian Literature* (DLT)

Celtic Parables (SPCK)

Collins Gem Book of Prayers (HarperCollins)

Celtic Gifts

Orders of ministry in the Celtic Church

Robert Van de Weyer

CANTERBURY
PRESS
Norwich

© Robert Van de Weyer, 1997

First published in 1997 by The Canterbury Press Norwich
(a publishing imprint of Hymns Ancient & Modern Limited
a registered charity)
St Mary's Works, St Mary's Plain
Norwich, Norfolk, NR3 3BH

British Library Cataloguing in Publication Data

A catalogue record for this book is available
from the British Library

ISBN 1-85311-158-9

Typeset by Rowland Phototypesetting and printed in Great Britain by
St Edmundsbury Press, Bury St Edmunds, Suffolk

PREFACE

This is the story of an event which has yet to take place: the transformation of a diocese within the Church of England along Celtic lines. It is not simply the mechanics of this process which are interesting, but the thoughts and feelings which inspire and guide it. Thus much of the book is taken up with the conversations of those charged with leading the transformation. They do not always see eye to eye; but then the genius of the Church of England is to use its disputes and disagreements creatively. And that genius is rooted in its ancient Celtic history.

CONTENTS

PROLOGUE

Gyrwas Diocese and Bishop Tom Birt

In the 1980s there was a surge of interest amongst British people in their distant Celtic past. Tourist sites associated with Celtic heroes and saints attracted tens of thousands of extra visitors. Greetings cards showing Celtic knotwork were sent to mark birthdays and anniversaries. There were even Celtic theme weddings, in which bride and groom dressed like their ancient forebears. And books with 'Celtic' in the title enjoyed remarkable sales.

This interest in the Celts embraced both Christians and those without formal faith. And since Christianity had come to Britain during the Celtic period, both groups could find literature and art to suit their tastes. But it was amongst Christians that the Celtic revival was most marked. As they read the stories of the Celtic saints and the churches they founded, they saw a style of religion which seemed free, light of heart, joyful – and hence wonderfully attractive. Despite their own tenacious commitment to Christianity, many Christians had lost confidence in their religion as a purveyor of spiritual and moral truth to the world, and as a sign of hope. Celtic Christianity offered a vision which renewed their confidence.

At the same time the main Christian institutions in Britain entered a period of crisis. At first most leaders were complacent, believing that the antiquity of their churches would protect them from serious danger. But as the years passed, it became increasingly clear that the very existence of some denominations was under threat; and that none could survive in their present form.

The crisis was most visible in the Church of England. Historically this was the largest denomination in Britain, with the greatest number of church buildings, and it played the greatest part in national life. Although many English

1

people felt a lingering attachment to the Church of England, the number of regular worshippers had steadily dwindled to a tiny proportion of the population. And the material assets had also dwindled, both through mismanagement and through wider economic forces. Since these assets had been the main source of income for the clergy, the dioceses – which were responsible for paying the clergy – had no choice but to demand much larger amounts from the local congregations. Initially congregations met these demands quite willingly. But as the sums required continued to grow, as the cost of maintaining their ancient church buildings got no smaller, and as congregations in many places continued to fall – then churches in increasing numbers started to default.

By the mid 1990s, some dioceses were facing the possibility of running out of cash, and thence being unable to pay their clergy. Bishops saved the situation by long delays in replacing clergy who had retired or moved on. And in order to set diocesan finances back on firm ground, they made large cuts in clergy numbers, especially in rural areas, amalgamating ever-larger groups of parishes under a single vicar. Some congregations, which had coped without a vicar for two or three years, or who rarely saw the vicar they did have, began to wonder whether vicars in the traditional sense were really needed. And in most parishes throughout the country fund-raising, in order to meet the diocesan demands for cash, had become the major single activity. Even the clergy, for whose sake these efforts were being made, felt trapped: they were spending more and more of their time in organizing fund-raising events, to raise money for the dioceses to pay their salaries – in order to organize more fund-raising events.

* * * * *

In January of the year 2000 a new bishop, Tom Birt, was appointed to the Diocese of Gyrwas. Tom Birt knew Gyrwas well, having served as vicar in one of its more remote rural areas before being appointed as archdeacon elsewhere; so

2

he quickly familiarized himself with the current state of affairs. The southern half of Gyrwas is almost entirely flat, with large open fields growing vegetables and grain; and the city of Gyrwas is in the midst of this vast expanse, standing on an outcrop of gravel; its tall slender spire has miraculously withstood seven centuries of wind and rain. The northern half is gently rolling countryside, with sheep and cattle vastly outnumbering humans; in the north-western corner is the prosperous university town of Kimford, which now contains hundreds of small high-tech businesses.

Although there are pockets of poverty, Gyrwas as a whole is one of the most prosperous areas of Britain. Yet the material problems of the Church of England were as acute here as anywhere. In the previous two centuries, since the industrial and agricultural revolutions, the population of many of the villages had fallen to one or two hundred; and in most only a handful attended church on a Sunday. So the double burden of maintaining an ancient church building, and of meeting the diocese's demands, had become impossible for many parishes. Some were failing to meet these demands, and most were delaying repairs to their church's fabric. At the reception after his enthronement as Bishop of Gyrwas Cathedral, Tom Birt was accosted by a churchwarden from one of his former parishes. 'If I were a young man today,' the old farmer said, 'I wouldn't bother with church. All this fund-raising uses up every minute of your spare time. And what do you get for it? Just more grey hairs.'

As a vicar in Gyrwas Diocese in the 1980s, Tom Birt had been intrigued by the Celtic revival, and he had purchased some of the books about the Celts which had flooded the Christian bookshop in his town. He had even used stories of the Celtic saints in some of his sermons, and had been surprised at the positive response, even from the horny-handed farmers. As archdeacon he had organized two conferences on Celtic Christianity, which had been hugely over-booked – a rarity for any Christian event. Before his enthronement Tom Birt had been visited by the diocesan treasurer, who alerted him to their dire financial state. And once he began to visit parishes and meet the congregations, he found that almost every conversation sooner or later turned to money. He began to wonder whether the ancient Celts might have something to say to this grim situation.

Tom Birt's predecessor had been a theologian, who had arranged for every wall of his large study to be lined with bookshelves. Tom Birt's modest library barely occupied one wall, and he filled the rest with knick-knacks, photographs and files. But he was quietly proud of his collection of Celtic books, which occupied three complete shelves. And in the autumn he took the books down one by one, browsing through their pages in search of guidance. Despite his love for ancient church buildings, he envied the Celts' lack of these expensive spiritual ornaments. Like many church leaders in modern times, he was tempted with the idea of abandoning them, and urging people to worship in each other's homes. But then he read of the respect which the Celtic Christians had for ancient Druid shrines – and of how they converted these shrines into churches.

* * * * *

Early one Friday morning in November, before the round of meetings and interviews had begun, he found himself reflecting on the Celts' style of ministry. Again like many church leaders in modern times, he had long deplored the Church's dependence on ordained clergy, and as an arch-deacon he had organized numerous courses for training lay people in Christian ministry. But after all this effort, few of these lay people took over any of the vicar's work, or developed independent ministries of their own; at most they became a little more articulate at church meetings. The problem, Tom Birt had concluded, lay in the personalities of the clergy themselves: they were frightened of allowing lay people to take positions of spiritual prominence, for fear of being outshone. This morning, however, Tom Birt saw the issue in a new light. The Celtic churches did not have just one leader, but many leaders; indeed they strived to

4

make everyone into a spiritual leader. And they recognized that there are many different types and gifts of leadership – so the exercise of one kind of ministry did not threaten those exercising another kind.

At first Tom Birt felt excited at this insight, as if it were entirely fresh. Later, as he lingered over a cup of coffee between interviews, he realized that the same point had been made by every lecturer at every lay training course he had put on; the only difference was that none of the lecturers had referred to the Celts. In fact they had usually pointed to an even higher authority, the epistles of St Paul, which contain several lists of the various gifts and ministries within the Church, and seem to suggest that every believer possesses at least one spiritual gift. Tom Birt felt a little flat at his lack of originality; yet somehow he sensed that there was something special in the Celtic view of ministry – and that his earlier elation arose because of this intuition.

At three o'clock that afternoon Tom Birt had to interview a woman in her early thirties who felt called to the priesthood. The Director of Ordinands had referred her upwards to the bishop, because he was perplexed by her. As he wrote in his brief report, 'I sense she would make a superb preacher, but would be a disaster in charge of a parish.' After half an hour in her company, Tom Birt felt quite inspired by her fluency, her vivid language, and her evident understanding of spiritual matters – indeed, a potentially excellent preacher who should have a place in the pulpits of Gyrwas Diocese. But he also felt a little wary, almost frightened of her; a deep, even violent anger seemed to lurk just below the surface of her charismatic personality. He too was perplexed. He agreed that she would make a terrible pastor. Yet her ability to express, even to radiate, the Christian faith, could attract large numbers back into the Church – and not to ordain her would deprive the Church of this ability.

After she had left, his secretary brought him a pot of tea, to refresh him before his next interview – another look at the diocesan accounts with the treasurer. 'Yes,' he whispered to himself out loud as he supped the tea, 'I know what was special about Celts.' Paul had affirmed the multiplicity of gifts; the Celtic bishops actually ordained and authorized the people who possessed them. At most the pastors of the local churches may have co-ordinated the various gifts and ministries. But the roving bishops picked out people possessing those gifts, often took them away for training and guidance, and then ordained them to exercise their gifts to the full.

Tom Birt rang the diocesan office, and asked the treasurer to delay his visit for half an hour. He poured himself another cup, and reflected on which gifts seemed to flourish in the Celtic churches, and which of the saints exercised and exemplified each gift. Within a few minutes he had identified six, including that of bishop. And the idea came into his head that he should start within Gyrwas six 'Orders', named after the relevant saint. He would invite people to offer themselves for at least one of these Orders: their vocation would be tested, and suitable training given; and then he would ordain them.

Throughout his meeting with the diocesan treasurer Tom Birt was unable to concentrate on the latest income and expenditure figures. Fortunately the treasurer was undeterred by Tom Birt's disinterest, since the primary purpose of the meeting was for the treasurer himself to feel satisfied that he 'was keeping the Bishop fully informed of the situation' – the fact that the Bishop could not absorb the information was secondary. None the less, Tom Birt's mind was on money: he was wondering about the financial implications of the Celtic model of ministry. Clearly if it did not solve the present financial dilemma, or even made it worse, it would be utterly irrelevant. But if it offered dramatic reductions in diocesan expenditure, the financial crisis would be seen as an opportunity sent by God to make such radical changes. 'Crisis,' he reminded himself from his studies of New Testament Greek, means 'judgement'; and 'radical' means 'returning to one's roots'. The Church of England's crisis, he mused, could be God's judgement on her style of ministry and mission, prompting her to return to her roots.

It was not until the treasurer's lengthy report had finished that Tom Birt was able to think through a Celtic approach to money. He poured himself a sherry, and propped himself on the sill of the medieval window of his study, overlooking his walled garden. It was now dark, but the cathedral flood-lights beyond his wall made silhouettes of his trees. In Celtic times, he thought, no one had full-time jobs, but people did a variety of tasks which yielded a material return. Presumably those people who devoted a large part of their time to Christian ministry received food and drink from the people to whom they ministered; and, as various stories illustrate, those ministering in poor or hostile areas received material help from churches elsewhere who wanted to support them. Most ministry, however, was done in people's spare time, after the crops and the animals had been tended.

In a strange way, Tom Birt reflected, our pattern of living has come full circle. Again many people do not have single jobs with a single employer, but do two, three or even several tasks for different employers and clients, being paid for their work task by task; and they must be ready to acquire new skills as required. So it would be quite possible for a few people to exercise a Christian ministry as one of their tasks – and, if necessary, to be paid for what they do by the church where they minister. Equally, as in Celtic times, most ministry would be done in people's spare time; and our present more flexible forms of employment would make it easier for people – if they could make the financial sacrifice – to create a little more spare time. The role of the bishop in all this – as in Celtic times – would be to provide whatever training and continuing guidance was necessary. And for this the diocese would have to ask churches to make a contribution, like a membership fee; but the amount would be a tiny fraction of the present financial demands. The bishop would also encourage more prosperous churches to support Christian ministry in the poorer areas – just as Paul urged the Corinthians to support the Judaean church.

* * * * *

Even as these ideas formed in Tom Birt's mind, he could hear the objections. The diocesan treasurer, and the other diocesan officials, would worry about loss of central control, claiming that parishes would be very inefficient and wasteful if they paid directly for ministry. This would be easy to counter. Until little over half a century ago, parishes in England organized their own finances and managed their own material assets perfectly well – as they continue to do in virtually every other part of the Anglican Communion across the world. Besides, people will give far more generously to parish funds if they themselves control the use of this money. Tom Birt could also hear his old churchwarden grumbling about the church taking over even more of his spare time. But surely people would derive great satisfaction from exercising their spiritual gifts, rather than organizing countless jumble sales.

The greatest anxieties, however, would come from the parish clergy themselves. The Celtic model would mean an end to secure life-time employment for people in dog collars. Yet, as many recognize, this security is already under grave threat. As one of Gyrwas's archdeacons said at the last diocesan synod, the diocese is only obliged by law to pay a tiny fraction of the clergy salaries, based on an arcane calculation made long ago – and even this applies only to those clergy with the 'freehold' on their parishes. The archdeacon went on to say that, in the event of the diocese running out of cash, parishes would have to make a direct financial arrangement with their clergy. This statement was intended to frighten parishes into meeting the diocese's financial demands; and some clergy indeed reacted with fear. But in conversation afterwards Tom Birt was surprised at how many people, both clergy and lay people, welcomed the idea of a personal contract between priest and parish. As one vicar, ministering to eight tiny villages, said to Tom Birt: 'My people wouldn't let me starve.'

Tom Birt cast his mind back to his own days as priest in a remote patch of Gyrwas, and remembered his intense frustration at much of what he was required to do. He hated the administration, and was not especially good at visiting the sick. But, like the woman whom he had interviewed that afternoon, he was a natural preacher, and loved leading study groups. How much happier he would have been if the system had allowed him to concentrate on his preaching and teaching ministry, perhaps combining it with part-time work teaching mathematics – his original degree subject – in a local school or college. Other priests are mediocre preachers, and even dread their weekly excursion into the pulpit, but are excellent pastors, bringing hope and encouragement wherever they go. And a surprisingly large number of priests are highly efficient and capable administrators. Surely most, like him, would actually want to belong to an order where they could specialize in the tasks for which God had called them, and leave the rest to others. Some large parishes in cities like Kimford, or groups of parishes in the countryside, would probably want to employ one or two full-time ministers – a pastor, perhaps, and even an administrator. Others would prefer to depend on part-time and spare-time ministers. Under the Celtic system they would be free to choose – just as an ordinary business chooses how to employ the people it needs.

With a second glass of sherry, Tom Birt's mind pushed on to wider matters. A major stimulus to the Celtic revival in recent years has been the emphasis in Celtic poetry on the presence of God in every person and every living creature, and thence on the mutual dependence of all creatures. Thus in many people's eyes the Celtic saints are the spiritual patrons of the Green movement in politics. The Celtic model of ministry, Tom Birt reflected, is the application of the same idea to the Church itself: God's spiritual gifts are bestowed on everyone, and the total ministry and mission of the Church depends on all people exercising their gifts. Despite the best efforts of modern bishops and clergy to pretend otherwise, the Church is still seen by both members and outsiders as a pyramid, with the bishop at the apex, the clergy in the middle, and the laity at the bottom. Celtic ministry is a circle, or, more precisely, a circular chain: every link, including that of the bishop's ministry, is equal; and all links are vital. If the diocese of Gyrwas is to become

Celtic, Tom Birt reflected, the financial adjustments will be the easy part; instilling a true sense of equality will be much harder.

*   *   *   *   *

Before his enthronement Tom Birt had promised his wife that they would continue to go shopping together every Saturday morning, as they had done for the past thirty years of their marriage. And since January they had gone each week to a large wholefood warehouse on the edge of Kimford, run as a co-operative by disabled people. But this Saturday he asked his wife if they could postpone their trip, to spend the morning together studying Celtic saints. The next diocesan synod was only a fortnight away; and in his opening address he wanted to outline his Celtic revolution, to see how people reacted. And, if it gained a favourable response, he could form a sub-committee of his Bishop's Council to work out detailed proposals, which could be discussed at length in every parish.

By lunchtime Tom Birt and his wife had decided what the various orders of ministry should be, and who should be the patron saints. Two weeks later he described his vision of a Celtic diocese to the clergy and laity who gathered in Gyrwas cathedral. Some were anxious; some confused; a few felt angry. But most were cautiously warm. During the early months of 2001 Tom Birt and his sub-committee tried to distil the Celtic vision into a set of proposals which parishes could debate, and then accept or reject. But to their frustration they found that the vision defied such precision. Eventually they concluded that only as the vision was enacted would its meaning and implications become clear.

Thus at the diocesan synod in the summer of 2001 the sub-committee proposed that, one by one, each Order should be founded with only a small number of members. These founding members would then discuss, in the light of the life and teaching of their patron saint, the nature of their particular ministry, and how their Order should operate in view of this. Then, as they themselves became clear about the way forward, they would report to Tom Birt; and between them they would communicate with the diocese as a whole.

They decided that the first Order to be founded should be the Order of St Aidan, named after the first Celtic bishop in England. Tom Birt invited the suffragan bishop and the three archdeacons to join him.

1. BISHOPS

The Order of St Aidan

The Order of St Aidan was founded on 31 August, the Saint's traditional feast day, 2001. The five founding members felt acutely nervous, recognizing that this was the first step in a long and momentous journey, at the end of which Gyrwas Diocese would be utterly transformed. None the less they decided the service inaugurating the Order should be quiet and unspectacular: it took place in a side chapel of Gyrwas Cathedral, with only a small number of invited guests. As Tom Birt said in his sermon, the Order of bishops must be the smallest of the six Orders, and should be regarded as the least important.

In addition to their usual meetings to discuss diocesan affairs, the five of them decided to meet once a fortnight for the next four months, to learn about St Aidan, and to determine how they could serve Gyrwas Diocese according to his spirit and example.

* * * * *

Aidan came to northern England at the invitation of the young king, Oswald, who was already familiar with the Christian faith. Oswald asked the monks of Iona, the monastery founded by Columba on a Scottish island, if they would send one of their number to come and preach the gospel. Initially they sent a stern and austere monk who antagonized the Northumbrians. After several months without a single convert, he returned to Iona and reported that the Northumbrians were too obstinate and barbarous to receive the Christian faith. So the abbot called the monks together to decide what should be done. Some agreed that any further efforts would be fruitless, and so they should abandon the Northumbrians to the devil. But others felt deeply upset at such a hard-hearted attitude. Finally Aidan, one of the youngest monks, spoke up. 'Brother,' he said to the man whose mission had failed, 'it seems to me that you were too severe with your hearers. You should have followed the example of Christ and the apostles, who began by giving people the milk of simple teaching, gradually nourishing them with the Word of God until they were capable of greater perfection.' There was silence as the monks absorbed Aidan's words. Then the abbot turned to Aidan, and pronounced that he was clearly the right person to undertake the mission to Northumbria, since he was especially endowed with 'discretion, the mother of all virtues'.

One of the archdeacons, from the northern part of Gyrwas, suggested with a smile that the conference at Iona contains one obvious truth, which every church council member rapidly learns: if you make a suggestion, you are liable to be asked to carry it out. But the deeper question, they all agreed, was what Aidan meant by 'milk', and what the abbot meant by 'discretion'. The suffragan bishop observed that when Jesus and the apostles went from village to village, they were speaking to 'obstinate and barbarous people' like the Northumbrians; and Jesus even thanked the Father that his message was more easily received by such people, than by those whose minds were filled with theology and philosophy. As the gospel accounts make clear, they avoided all kinds of religious jargon and abstract intellectual concepts; instead they conveyed their message in witty sayings and stories. 'So you could say,' the suffragan concluded, 'that they were "discreet" in their use of language; and as a result their words were easily digested like mother's milk.'

'But does that mean,' the archdeacon from the southern part of Gyrwas asked, 'that Jesus and the apostles were giving people a childish version of the truth, rather than the real thing? To extend Aidan's metaphor, do we grow out of the milk of simple stories, and move on to the red meat of theology?' Tom Birt smiled, pointing out that he alone in the group did not have a university degree in theology: 'So I'm still on mother's milk.' There was a long silence. Then the archdeacon from central Gyrwas said that mother's milk contains all the nutrients needed for physical survival and growth; in the same way, the teachings of Jesus and the apostles recorded in the New Testament contain all we need for spiritual growth. 'So what is the point of theology?' the northern archdeacon asked. 'Theology, as the word implies, is our reflection on the truth,' the central archdeacon replied, 'not the truth itself.'

'The trouble is,' said the suffragan, 'when people like us in dog collars climb into the pulpit to preach, we are much more comfortable talking about theology, than telling witty stories. Words like "redemption", "incarnation" and "justification" trip off our tongues – as if people's souls could be saved by understanding what they mean.' The central archdeacon suggested that they all try to wean themselves in reverse, giving up the red meat of theology and using only mother's milk. Thus whenever one of them in their meetings used a theological term or abstract concept, the others should interrupt, demanding that 'milky' terms be used instead – and if milky terms could not be found, the idea should be rejected as nonsensical.

The next three or four sessions after imposing this discipline on themselves were like prolonged parlour games, in which they each had to guard what they said in case the others caught them out. And they felt horribly self-conscious outside the sessions, tying themselves into verbal knots to avoid theological jargon. Yet to their surprise their thoughts and reflections on their faith gradually became clearer, and they found themselves speaking more fluently.

*   *   *   *   *

When Aidan arrived in Northumbria and began touring its villages and farms, he quickly won people's hearts. And the richer folk showed their appreciation – perhaps also trying to gain divine approval – by giving him money. Oswald himself wanted to build a fine house for Aidan. But Aidan believed that a bishop should have no involvement with financial affairs, since money would soon taint the purity of his teaching, and undermine his authority. So he either refused to accept gifts, or immediately passed them on to the poor, or in some cases used the gifts to ransom men who had been unjustly imprisoned. As a result he felt free to visit the rich people of Northumbria, and speak frankly to them about their abuses of wealth and power. And to the delight and gratitude of the poor, he persuaded many to change their ways.

Tom Birt said that since he became bishop, the financial problems of the diocese had felt like a huge burden weighing on his shoulders, which he longed to shake off. And, even if he tried to forget about it, the grumbling lay people in every parish he visited would soon remind him. 'In the nine years that I have been in this job,' the northern archdeacon said, 'the burden has got heavier and heavier.' And he added that they, as bishops and archdeacons, were caught in an impossible dilemma. On the one hand they had had no training in financial management, and probably no aptitude either. Yet on the other hand, the current system demanded that they act as the board of directors of a large institution, whose main practical function was to collect money from one group of people, the laity, and hand it on to another group, the clergy.

'But is our message tainted by money?' the suffragan asked. 'I doubt if any of us,' replied the central archdeacon, 'have ever deliberately slanted our words to flatter or appease the rich. Nor do we join golf clubs or attend civic receptions in order to beg money from local businessmen.' 'Yes, that's true,' responded the northern archdeacon, 'but whenever we preach in a parish church, the people in the pews know the score – that more than anything else the diocese needs their money. And, if we're honest, we know this compromises our authority. When I started out as archdeacon, I often preached quite challenging sermons; I even once spoke against fox-hunting in a village where hounds were kept. Not now: I've become soft and bland, so as not to upset anybody.' 'There's now an eleventh commandment,' said the suffragan, 'especially written for bishops and archdeacons: "Thou shalt be nice at all times."'

'There's another reason to free ourselves from financial concerns,' said Tom Birt, 'they take up so much time.' They tried to add up all the hours they spent, directly or indirectly, on money. There were committee meetings and interviews specifically about finances. There were meetings with local clergy, in which the conversation almost invariably turned to the financial anxieties and to their parishes' problems in meeting the diocese's demands. And there were conversations with lay people at parish events that were often similarly blighted. Even their regular meetings as a group to discuss clergy vacancies were increasingly dominated by financial considerations. The question 'Can we afford to fill this vacancy?' was as common as 'What is the right kind of priest for this parish?' 'I reckon,' concluded the northern archdeacon, 'the black cloud of money hangs over almost half our daily activities.'

Tom Birt said that he had inherited from his predecessors a small 'discretionary fund' in which gifts from well-wishers were put; he could then make payments to people in need within the diocese. 'Should I keep this fund going?' he asked. 'Emphatically yes,' said the suffragan, 'it's the only type of financial involvement consistent with the spirit of Aidan.' Apart from this fund, the group decided that, whatever else happened in the reorganization of Gyrwas Diocese, they would publicly and firmly renounce all financial responsibilities; and they would refuse to engage in any conversations or discussions about diocesan financial affairs.

*   *   *   *   *

When Aidan arrived in Northumbria, King Oswald wanted his new bishop to behave in a grand and regal manner. He offered Aidan fine clothes to wear, like those of a royal prince. But Aidan insisted on wearing a rough woollen tunic, like that of a peasant. He also wanted the new bishop to travel around his diocese on horseback; and he gave Aidan one of his finest stallions for the purpose. A good horse, Oswald argued, would enable Aidan to travel faster and so reach more places; it would be more comfortable, and prevent Aidan's robes getting dirty from the muddy lanes; and, most important of all, it would reflect the dignity and status of his position. But Aidan immediately gave the stallion to a beggar, and insisted on travelling always on foot. In this way he could meet and talk to other travellers, telling them about the gospel as they walked. Besides, Aidan said, a bishop should speak to his people

as an equal – as a fellow sinner in need of God's grace. Oswald
was initially offended at Aidan's rejection of his gift. 'I possess
many other less valuable horses that are good enough for the poor,'
the king testily remarked. 'You seem to be saying,' replied Aidan,
'that your stallion is more valuable to you than the poor child of
God to whom I gave it.' There was a pause, and then Oswald
threw himself at Aidan's feet and begged forgiveness.

Aidan's victory was short-lived. A few decades later the Bishop
of Lichfield, called Chad, tried to model himself on Aidan, insisting
that he toured his diocese in the west Midlands on foot. But the
new Archbishop of Canterbury, Theodore, who had been sent by
the Pope to reform the English church on Roman lines, ordered
Chad to travel only on horseback. And from that moment onwards
bishops in Britain moved from place to place in aristocratic style.

'I'm afraid that a modern bishop plodding across a scattered
rural diocese,' said the northern archdeacon, 'would meet
almost no one, so the gesture would be entirely wasted.
Perhaps we could travel occasionally by bus, to meet poorer
and older people who can't afford cars.' The southern archdeacon said that the mode of transport was not the point
of the story: 'In my view Aidan was saying something
important about the function of bishops. Oswald and
Theodore believed that bishops should visit as many places
as possible, conducting services and attending meetings of
local leaders. Aidan believed that bishops should meet as
many people as possible – and that they should mix with
those at the bottom of society, just as much as with those
at the top.'

At the suffragan's suggestion, the five of them took out
their diaries, to look at their programmes of engagements.
They could see that their days and evenings were filled with
meetings, services and social events where they mixed with
clergy and secular leaders of various kinds, and where the
conversations with ordinary churchgoers were mostly
stilted and artificial. They rarely met those from the majority
of the population, who neither attended church nor had
positions of eminence in the world. 'We are playing by
Theodore's rules, not by Aidan's,' the suffragan concluded.

'The solution is simple,' said Tom Birt. 'We reduce

drastically the number of events in our diaries and increase hugely the length of each visit we make around Gyrwas. Instead of driving out to a parish for an individual service or meeting, and then rushing home, we will ask to spend two or three nights in a parish. Then we'll have time to wander round chatting to people in the street and knocking on doors – getting round on foot, like Aidan.' The central archdeacon took a small calculator from his wallet, and worked out that if they each visited fifteen parishes, or groups of parishes, each year, they could get round the whole of Gyrwas once every two years.

'Aidan is also saying something important about the status of bishops,' said the suffragan. 'Those wonderful robes which Tom Birt and I wear at services are really royal robes. In fact bishops are the only people left who still wear royal regalia – the real royal family wears normal clothes for most functions. And, of course, the purple shirts we wear all the time now have royal connotations. Aidan by contrast refused all outside sign of privilege.' 'So why do you wear all that stuff?' the northern archdeacon asked with a smile. 'Not because I enjoy it,' replied the suffragan. 'I suppose it's because I would offend people if I didn't. Churchgoers like to see their bishops strutting round like princes.' 'You don't actually know that,' said the northern archdeacon, 'and even if they told you they liked it, all you'd learn is that churchgoers like tradition. But traditions can change.' 'Yes, I agree,' said the suffragan, 'I'm not trying to defend my silly clothes. I'm expressing unease. And I know that my clothes make a lot of people treat me with a kind of nervous awe – even some of the clergy.'

'So what is the modern equivalent of Aidan's rough woollen tunic?' the southern archdeacon asked. Then he suggested his own answer: 'For men, a shirt and sometimes a tie, a sweater, perhaps a jacket, jeans or trousers. For women much the same, except no tie, and perhaps a skirt instead of trousers.' 'But that's much the same as we wear now,' said the northern archdeacon, 'except that we have a dog collar instead of a tie.' 'It's you two bishops who have got to change,' concluded the central archdeacon. 'Get rid

of your royal purple shirts, and your royal robes for services
– and dress like the other clergy.'

*　*　*　*　*

*Soon after arriving in Northumbria, Aidan built a hut for himself
in Lindisfarne, a small island a few hundred yards from the coast,
which can be reached on foot across the sands at low tide. When
people became Christians, he invited them to Lindisfarne to learn
more about their faith and to develop their spiritual gifts. He then
authorized them to exercise their gifts in their own locality, and
sent them home. As the Church in Northumbria grew, Aidan
recruited others to share this work of guiding and training the
faithful; and by the time of his death Lindisfarne had become a
large community.*

'Should we have a Gyrwas Lindisfarne, where people come
to train for ministry?' the central archdeacon asked. At first
the group warmed to the idea. They calculated that the cost
of running a diocesan training college for ministry would
impose only a modest financial burden on parishes; and
since parishes would no longer have to meet the much
larger financial demands from the diocese, they might be
willing to carry this. Then they began to plan how the college would operate: the staff it would need; the courses it
would run; and the buildings it would use. The five of them
became increasingly excited.

But the northern archdeacon punctured their enthusiasm
with a simple question: 'Who would be in charge of this
thing?' There was a pause. Then the suffragan offered an
answer: 'Presumably Aidan was in charge of Lindisfarne; so
we would be in charge of this college.' 'But do you really
want to run a great college?' the northern archdeacon persisted. 'We'll be administrators all over again, worrying
about money,' agreed the suffragan.

'Yes,' said the southern archdeacon, 'we've been missing
the point. Lindisfarne can't have been like a modern college,
with courses, timetables and the rest; and Aidan can't have
been like a modern vice-chancellor.' 'So how was it run?'
the suffragan asked. 'I suspect we can answer that question,'

Tom Birt replied, 'by asking another question: Who are the right people to train pastors, preachers and the rest? The answer is that pastors are the right people to train pastors; preachers should train preachers – and so on. So Aidan probably got good pastors, preachers, healers, artists and administrators to come and stay at Lindisfarne for a period; and then others could come and learn from them.'

'So I come back to where we started,' the central archdeacon persisted. 'Do we need a Gyrwas Lindisfarne?' 'Probably not,' said Tom Birt, 'but it's not for us to decide. Each Order will have to make its own arrangements for training. And if together they decide to combine in having one big training centre, so be it. If not, then there may be lots of mini Lindisfarnes. It's the activity, not the place, which matters.'

* * * * *

Tom Birt and his suffragan bishop abandoned their purple shirts for the first time at the diocesan synod in December 2001, appearing in grey shirts like the rest of the clergy. The suffragan gave a speech, outlining their reflections about St Aidan and their plans for imitating him in their own ministry. He did not mention their change of dress; but this was the main topic of conversation in the coffee break.

2. PASTORS

The Order of St Cuthbert

The Order of St Cuthbert was formed on 20 March, the saint's traditional feast day, 2002. In Tom Birt's view Cuthbert exemplified the pastor, who nurtured and guided those in his care. As a monk at Melrose, on the border of Scotland and England, and later at Lindisfarne, he acted as pastor of the villages and homesteads around the monasteries; and as prior of Lindisfarne, he showed great pastoral skill with the monks. Thus he was the appropriate patron of pastors in Gyrwas Diocese.

Tom Birt invited five experienced vicars to be the founding members of the Order. One was a man in his early sixties, who had been ordained as a young man forty years earlier; he now had charge of four rural parishes near Gyrwas itself. The second was a woman in her late fifties, who had been ordained only ten years earlier, having been a schoolteacher before; she had a suburban parish in an industrial town at the south-west corner of the diocese. The third was a woman aged thirty, who had just become vicar in a suburb of Kimford. The fourth was a single man in his early forties, who openly described himself as a 'celibate gay'; he also had a parish on the outskirts of Kimford. The fifth was a man in his early fifties, who had been ordained twenty years earlier, and had served since then as the unpaid vicar of two remote rural parishes, earning his living as an accountant.

In all five cases their parishes, or groups of parishes, had responded immediately to the Celtic scheme by saying that they wanted to retain their present pastoral arrangements – and that, in the first four cases, the parishes would raise enough money to pay their vicar's salary. Following the example of Tom Birt and his companions, the five began to meet each fortnight, to study the life of St Cuthbert and reflect on their own experience, in order to work out the specific role of the pastor in the circular chain of ministry – and by inference the roles that do not belong to the pastor, but to other ministries.

* * * * *

As a child Cuthbert was an enthusiastic and agile sportsman, who could beat the boys of his own age, and also many grown men, at wrestling, jumping and running. And although he came from an educated and devout family, he was lazy at his books and indifferent to religion. His conversion was triggered by a small boy, apparently only three or four years old, reprimanding him for wasting his time on frivolous games, when he should be 'learning to control his body and mind for the service of God.' And as soon as he reached adulthood Cuthbert crossed the Cheviot hills to Melrose to offer himself as a monk. But the recollection of his idle childhood, and of the divine grace he received through the small boy, freed him from any inclination to stand in judgement over the sins and failures of others.

Thus when he began visiting the people living around Melrose, they felt able to speak with him freely. Other monks whom they had met had seemed stern and severe, chastising them for their immoral ways; so they naturally held their tongues whenever a monk appeared, for fear of provoking further angry words. But Cuthbert's gentle manner and his humility loosened their tongues. So soon, wherever he went people asked to speak to him privately, and they opened their hearts to him. Cuthbert listened with great care, asking questions so that he could understand fully what burdened them; then he would offer some simple piece of advice.

Despite Cuthbert's humility and gentleness, the oldest vicar wondered whether Cuthbert was a prig as a young man, doing more harm than good in the Melrose villages. He recalled with embarrassment his own moral zeal as a young priest: 'On one occasion I went to visit a woman who had three children by three different fathers; and I reduced her to tears by extolling the virtues of Christian marriage. Another time I told a young man who was suffering from depression that the cause of his illness was his refusal to let Jesus into his life. I threw velvet-covered bricks at people.'

'Does that mean that only older people, who have mellowed with the passing years, should serve as pastors?' asked the young woman vicar. 'Not at all,' said the ex-schoolteacher; 'I'm afraid I was just as ready to pass judgement on people when I first became a priest, and I already had grey hairs. Old people can be just as intolerant and condemning as young people – in some cases more so.' 'I think Cuthbert's problem,' said the gay vicar, 'is that he'd never really sinned. After all, a preference for sport over education is hardly very high in the catalogue of evil. In fact a boy who loathes sport, and spends all his time with his nose in a book, is probably in far greater danger. If he'd done some really juicy sins before he became a monk, I'm sure he would have been much nicer.'

'I think we're being a bit unfair to poor Cuthbert,' interjected the accountant. 'We don't know that he was a prig. In any case, you don't need to have committed a particular sin in order to be compassionate towards those who have. What matters is that you are aware of your own potential for evil: that in the wrong circumstances and with the wrong influences, you would be capable of committing any and every kind of sin. Self-knowledge, rather than personal experience, is the pastor's qualification.' 'So how do you acquire self-knowledge?' asked the young vicar. 'And how do you know when you've got enough to be a good pastor?' They all quickly agreed that none of them could claim sufficient self-knowledge to respond well to every situation. 'Fine,' persisted the young woman, 'but there are too many situations when I feel utterly inadequate. At the bedside of someone dying, after a bereavement or a messy divorce, even when a child has failed to get into the best local school – I just don't know what to say. And whatever I do say sounds horribly wrong.'

There was silence. Then the oldest vicar spoke: 'Our instinct is to try and solve people's problems; and we feel frustrated when we don't know how. But that's not our job; they must solve their own problems, or at least learn to cope with them. Our job is to listen to people with great care and compassion – so self-knowledge is important.

Through our listening, they learn to listen to themselves, and discover within their own souls the strength and wisdom they need.' There was a further silence. 'If so,' added the gay vicar, 'the best training for a pastor is to receive the care of a good pastor.'

*　*　*　*　*

After some years at Melrose, Cuthbert was invited to become Prior of Lindisfarne. Aidan had died about fifteen years earlier, and the common life at Lindisfarne had rapidly deteriorated. Many of the monks were not bothering to attend the services in the chapel which Aidan had built. They were going out into the local villages to beg for money, which they used to purchase the best food and clothes for themselves. And the distribution of this money between them was causing frequent quarrels, which often led to physical violence. A few monks were struggling to maintain the standards which Aidan had set; and they warmly welcomed Cuthbert, in the hope that he would restore the monastery to its former spiritual glory. But the majority were hostile, fearing that he would oppose their lax ways; and they took every opportunity to abuse him, shouting insults at him as he walked through the monastery grounds, and denouncing him at meetings.

Cuthbert never spoke against his opponents; he listened to their rude words, and remained silent. He visited their cells and engaged them in light-hearted conversation, never referring to problems in the community. And when any of them fell ill, he would stay at their bedside, nursing them and praying for their recovery. But despite his tolerance of the failings of others, Cuthbert himself followed Aidan's rules to the letter. He attended every service, he ate the simplest food, he dressed in a rough woollen tunic, he worked hard in the monastery garden – and, as at Melrose, he visited the surrounding villages to share the people's anxieties and fears. At first the monks at Lindisfarne mistook Cuthbert's tolerance for weakness, and gradually they stopped abusing him, believing that they could continue to misbehave with impunity. But eventually they recognized that his tolerance and gentleness were the signs of deep spiritual strength and serenity; and they started to envy these qualities, wanting to share them. So one by one they decided to imitate his way of life – until the entire community had returned to Aidan's path.

'Every vicar arriving in a parish,' said the ex-schoolteacher, 'faces Cuthbert's dilemma when he came to Lindisfarne, although it's usually much less acute. Some people want the new vicar to be a broom sweeping away all they disapprove of and dislike. Others are wary, fearing what the new vicar may do; and they make awkward, double-edged remarks.' 'I've been vicar in five different places,' said the oldest vicar, 'and I've always been greeted with the same mix of high expectation and deep dread. But I've found that if I mix happily with everybody, friend and foe alike, eventually things sort themselves out.' 'I'm afraid it's not as simple as that,' the gay vicar replied, 'you've got to make them believe in you as well. In my case there are always people wondering if I'm having lots of wild affairs and one-night stands. Only when they decide that I'm beyond reproach will they truly accept me as their pastor.' 'And what would happen if you had a steady partner?' asked the accountant. 'I could only be pastor to those who approved,' he replied.

'So what you're all saying,' exclaimed the young woman vicar, 'is that a pastor has to be nice to everyone all the time, and to be a moral paragon. That's impossible.' 'Put in that way, it is impossible,' agreed the ex-schoolteacher, 'but what we're really saying is that we must not burden people with our own problems and faults. Like it or not, the pastor more than anyone represents Christ. And since we can't be like Christ continually, we have to keep our distance. We can never make real friendships in our parishes, for fear that people will see us as we truly are.' 'So was Cuthbert putting on an act at Lindisfarne?' asked the young woman. 'Not an act,' replied the ex-schoolteacher, 'but showing only certain aspects of himself, I expect. In fact being a pastor and being a schoolteacher have a lot in common. You have to be sincere in front of a class; but you project the parts of yourself that are appropriate to that situation.'

'Okay,' said the young woman, 'you have to be pretty good and pretty nice. And you have to be a bit lonely as well. So who can judge themselves worthy, or even strong enough, to be pastors?' The oldest vicar observed that

Cuthbert never put himself forward as pastor: he was invited to be prior at Lindisfarne; and he later became bishop only after prolonged persuasion. 'Yet,' said the accountant, 'he must have thought that God wanted him to be a pastor, otherwise he would not have accepted the invitation. And that's the real dilemma of pastorship: particular individuals, like us, feel called by God to be pastors; yet, if the calling is genuine, we feel grossly unworthy of it.

* * * * *

Cuthbert believed that the roots of his pastoral ministry lay in prayer: this is the soil in which sympathy and understanding grow. And he seems to have needed very little sleep, so that he could devote much of the night to prayer. On one occasion at Melrose another monk saw Cuthbert rise from his bed in the small hours, and he followed Cuthbert down to the River Tweed. Cuthbert waded out into the river until the water came up to his neck, and remained there praying until dawn. He then came out of the water and lay on the bank. Two otters also emerged from the water and lay beside him, warming his feet with their breath and drying him by the heat of their bodies. When the otters had finished, Cuthbert blessed them, and they slipped back into the river. Cuthbert walked back to the monastery and joined the other monks in the chapel.

By the time he got to Lindisfarne Cuthbert was sleeping even less and praying more. He often stayed awake for three or four nights in a row, kneeling beside his bed. And when during the day the heaviness of sleep threatened to overcome him, he would go out into the garden to dig, or set off on a long walk to visit a village or a farm. One morning a monk complained to Cuthbert that another monk had kept him awake with loud snoring. 'Nobody can annoy me by keeping me awake,' replied Cuthbert, 'it lets me devote more time to God.' The bleary-eyed monk's response is not recorded.

'I'm afraid,' the gay vicar said, 'that I'm a flat-footed plodder, compared with the spiritual athleticism of Cuthbert. But I do know that prayer must be the root of my ministry, otherwise nothing will.' The oldest vicar took from his pocket a small computer, and pressed a few buttons to show a list of the people in his parishes whom he was praying for each day.

'I'm not as high-tech as you,' responded the young woman, and took out a small notebook containing the names of sick people. 'The actual connection of prayer to ministry is very mysterious,' said the accountant, 'since we're clearly not trying to nudge God's elbow. I imagine myself sitting with the people I'm praying for, as if I were visiting them.' 'And in a way,' said the oldest vicar, 'that's exactly what you are doing. If I've visited someone in my prayers, then I can listen to them much more compassionately in reality. The spiritual visit is like a preparation for the actual visit. And also prayer makes it much easier to love people you dislike.'

'It's a strange thing,' said the ex-schoolteacher, 'but even people who would never come to church, and who claim to be non-religious, seem to want me to pray for sick relatives and friends – and even for themselves when they fall sick.' The gay vicar suggested that people regard prayer as an act of love, and that pastors are valued above all as people of love. 'Does this mean,' asked the young woman, 'that in giving money for our salaries, people in reality are buying prayer? If so, it seems rather corrupt, like buying relics or indulgences.' 'Yes, I think that up to a point they are,' replied the ex-schoolteacher, 'but I don't think we need to feel ashamed of that. Prayer takes time. And when I was a busy schoolteacher I didn't have much time for prayer; so I was glad the vicar was praying on my behalf. Now it's the other way round.' 'But doesn't that encourage lay people to be lax in their prayers?' the young woman persisted. 'Perhaps,' said the oldest vicar, 'but you could regard paying hard-earned money for the vicar's salary as an act of prayer.' 'It all sounds rather self-serving to me,' the young woman replied.

'Let's put it another way,' said the gay vicar. 'Paying money for prayer has dangers. But refusing people's money would be even more dangerous. Those who happily support the pastor are not likely to pray more if the pastor disappears. And I believe that the pastor's prayer can uplift the entire spirit of a parish.' 'Oddly enough,' said the accountant, 'I agree. I don't actually ask for money. But I can only devote sufficient time to pray by working shorter hours. So I'm really paying for that time myself. I see no reason in principle why other people shouldn't chip in.'

* * * * *

Towards the end of his life Cuthbert decided to become a hermit on Farne Island, devoting even more time to prayer. The island is an outcrop of rock a few miles out to sea from Lindisfarne. At first Cuthbert depended on bread brought out on flimsy coracles by monks from Lindisfarne; but then he asked the monks to bring seed for him to sow on the thin soil of the island, so that he could be self-sufficient. When the seed began to ripen, birds flew down and began pecking it. 'Why are you eating crops you did not sow?' Cuthbert asked them. 'Is it that your need is greater than mine? If so, you have my permission to help yourselves; but if not, stop damaging what does not belong to you.'

The birds flew off. But three days later one of the birds returned. Cuthbert was harvesting his crop, and the bird landed in front of him, his feathers ruffled and his head drooping, as if to beg the saint's forgiveness. Cuthbert was overjoyed, blessing the bird, and inviting all of them to return. Back they came carrying a gift, a lump of pig's lard. Cuthbert kept it in the small guest-house he had built, inviting visitors to grease their shoes with it. 'If even the birds can show such humility and kindness,' Cuthbert would say, 'how much more we humans should seek such virtues.' The birds remained with Cuthbert, building their nests in the eaves of his cell; and he shared his barley with them.

'Of all the stories about Cuthbert,' said the gay vicar, 'the one that would most appeal to my parishioners is his friendship with the birds. That would prove that he was a good pastor.' 'I sometimes think,' added the ex-schoolteacher, 'that the reason why people in my parish have taken me to their hearts is that I have a house full of cats. And when I go to visit people in their homes, I always make a fuss of their pets.' 'In my experience,' said the oldest vicar, 'flowers and shrubs and trees fall in the same category. Admire someone's garden or their window-box, and they'll think you're a good sort.'

'Does that mean,' the young woman vicar asked, 'that we are supposed to be pastors of the animals and plants in our parishes, as well as the people?' The accountant replied that if he started talking to the local sparrows and pigeons in the manner of Cuthbert, the parishioners would conclude he was completely 'loopy', not just mildly so. 'None the less,' he added, 'I do believe that pastors should love and cherish all the living creatures in their parishes.' 'It's really a matter of theology,' said the gay vicar, 'of whether we regard the whole of God's creation as sacred. Too much Christian theology has concentrated on the human soul, as if it existed in a vacuum. But you can't separate the body from the soul; so Christianity must learn to love bodies as well as souls. And once you learn to love human bodies, you realize that you can't separate the body from the natural order as a whole. We're just one species amongst many – and all are sacred.'

'You're probably right,' said the oldest vicar, 'but it's all a bit complicated for me. All I know is that a good pastor is someone who enters the hearts of his or her people, and shares their concerns. And close to the hearts of most of my people are animals and plants.'

* * * * *

In August 2002 Tom Birt asked the five vicars if they were ready to extend the Order of St Cuthbert to include all in the diocese whom God was calling to be pastors. The five vicars replied that they were as ready as they ever would be. With Tom Birt's approval, they wrote a letter to every parish in Gyrwas, inviting people to put forward those whom they wished to be their pastors. They explained what they understood to be the pastor's role, in the light of their studies. And they said that the parishes were free to nominate whoever they felt had the spiritual gift of pastorship, and who were called to exercise that gift in their parish. In many cases this would be their existing vicar; but it might be one or more lay people whose gift had not yet been formally recognized. The smaller parishes were still free to form groups under a single pastor, or to have their own pastor. The letter reminded parishes that from now onwards the financial arrangements were entirely a matter for the parishes themselves: parishes could pay people to work full-time or part-time as pastors, or the pastors could serve freely in their spare time.

As for the training and testing of pastors, the letter said that, under the Celtic scheme which the diocese had adopted, this was now the responsibility of the Order itself. Initially the first five members would undertake these tasks – although in the case of most existing vicars, very little training and no testing would be needed. But as the Order expanded, the membership as a whole would choose its leaders. The letter concluded by saying that Bishop Tom Birt would ordain as pastors all who joined the Order, and that this would include ordination to the priesthood, so pastors would be authorized to conduct Communion services, as well as weddings, baptisms and funerals.

At the same time Tom Birt himself wrote to all the clergy in Gyrwas Diocese. He acknowledged that most of them faced a period of uncertainty, and that their future depended on two groups of people: the parishioners who had to decide whether to nominate them to one of the Orders, and also whether to pay a salary; and the relevant Order itself, which would decide whether to accept them. But this personal uncertainty was in reality a symptom of the financial crisis, which put a cloud of uncertainty over the entire diocese. From his personal knowledge of them, he believed that the majority were excellent pastors, and would thus become members of the Order of St Cuthbert. None the less, he urged all of them to reflect deeply on their spiritual gifts, and be open to the possibility that they might be called to other forms of ministry. And he suggested that they should look again at whether full-time Christian ministry really suited them, or whether they might be better ministers if they also had some secular employment.

The parishes had up to a year to reach a decision. Until they did so the diocese continued to pay their vicars, and they had to continue paying large sums to the diocese. In the meantime the Order of St Patrick was founded for the preaching ministry – which in the traditional English parish was also undertaken by the vicar.

3. PREACHERS

The Order of St Patrick

The Order of St Patrick was formed on 17 March 2003. The cathedral in Gyrwas was decked with shamrock for the inaugural service. In his sermon Tom Birt spoke of Patrick's extraordinary achievements as a preacher. Between his arrival at Strangford Lough, on the north-east coast of Ireland, in 435, and his death a quarter of a century later, he toured the island several times, speaking about the Christian faith to almost the entire population. And the great majority of those who heard him were persuaded by his eloquence, so that he could establish churches in every region. Patrick was the first of the great Celtic saints; and logically the Order dedicated to him should precede the Orders for bishops and pastors, since it is through preaching that people first encounter Christianity. But, whereas in Ireland in the fifth century the gospel was new, in Gyrwas at the start of the twenty-first century there is an ancient network of churches and congregations, that need to be supported and sustained. Nevertheless, Tom Birt concluded, the members of the Order of St Patrick will determine whether Christianity in Gyrwas survives and thrives in the future – or whether it continues its long, slow decline.

Five people joined the Order at the start, approved by Tom Birt. Two of them, a woman and a man, were vicars of parishes, and had already joined the Order of St Cuthbert, believing themselves to be gifted as pastors as well as preachers; and their parishes had concurred. The third had been vicar of a large and flourishing church in central Kimford. His inspirational sermons attracted huge numbers, especially students and other young people, but he regarded himself as a poor pastor. He had thus resigned as vicar, and his church had decided to support him as a full-time preacher. The fourth founder member of the Order was the diocesan missioner, who for the past five years had had a travelling ministry, preaching in churches and at rallies throughout Britain; he was supported by a special missionary trust which had been set up in Gyrwas in the nineteenth century. The fifth member was the young woman who had visited Tom Birt two and a half years ago, on the day when the idea of a Celtic diocese had first occurred to him. Tom Birt had seen her regularly since then, recommending books for her to read, and asking her to compose sermons; on several occasions he had arranged for her to preach in parish churches, where she had displayed great verve and eloquence.

The five of them began to study the life and the evangelistic techniques of their patron.

*   *   *   *   *

Uniquely among the Celtic saints, Patrick wrote his autobiography; our knowledge of the others comes from the works of admirers. His story begins with his capture as a teenage boy by pirates, who took him from his home on the west coast of Britain, and sold him as a slave to a sheep farmer in north-east Ireland. He was forced to live alone in a hut on a bleak hillside, staying with the sheep even in the most bitter winter weather. His initial despair lifted when he felt 'God's love fill my heart, and his Spirit warm my soul'. He started to pray almost continuously through the day, and often stayed awake at night to pray more. He remained on the mountain for six years, until one night he heard a voice, which told him that a ship was ready to take him back home. He immediately left the mountain and wandered through Ireland until he reached the south-east coast, where he persuaded the captain of a trading ship to take him on board.

But after the initial joy of seeing his parents again, he began to feel discontented and restless. He felt that God must have some special purpose for him, and he prayed for guidance. Then one night in a dream a man arrived from Ireland, imploring him to return there. And a few nights later he had another dream in which the man spoke again, asking him to go back to Ireland; and the man added, 'I am the one who laid down his life for you.' Patrick awoke convinced that Jesus himself was calling him back to Ireland to preach the gospel.

'So how did the call of Christ come to each of us?' asked the diocesan missioner. And he immediately gave his own answer. In words that he had repeated at many evangelistic rallies, he described how he had 'given my heart to Christ' at the age of twenty, after three years of promiscuity and drug-taking, and how as a result he was able to 'kick the heroin habit' without difficulty and to settle into a steady relationship with a girl, to whom he had now been happily married for over thirty years. 'Did you immediately take up preaching?' the woman vicar asked. This triggered another well-rehearsed soliloquy about an old friend from his pre-Christian days inviting him out for a drink in a pub, and how he managed to persuade both his friend and three other pub-goers to 'hand over their lives to Christ'.

The woman whom Tom Birt had nurtured had a more ambivalent tale, which she related with stuttering embarrassment. 'I've never spoken about all this in public,' she began. She told how she contracted anorexia after the sudden death of her mother, which gradually progressed into bulimia. 'Even today,' she confessed, 'I have occasional eating binges.' And she also described her persistent insomnia. She went on to speak of her mother's quiet, unshakeable faith in the love of God. 'One day in the psychiatric hospital I felt that my mother was very close, and she seemed to pass this faith from her soul to mine.' She concluded by saying that she in turn had a burning desire to pass this faith to others – 'even though I am a very poor example of how faith can improve your life'.

None of the others had stories as dramatic as these. But each could describe vividly the process by which they became 'a real Christian'; and each felt that the call to be a preacher was irresistible. 'The thing we have in common,' said the male vicar, 'is that we are very intense, emotional people – and, if we're honest, a bit unstable.' The preacher from the church in central Kimford bridled a little at being called unstable, but he recognized that his wife and children 'find me very hard to live with – which perhaps amounts to the same thing'.

* * * * *

Despite his conviction that Christ himself was calling him to Ireland, Patrick did not respond immediately. Most of the Irish people he had met seemed tough and harsh, and he himself was shy and ignorant; so the task of reaching their souls with the gospel of Christ was utterly beyond him. Moreover, he had no desire to return to the land where he had lived miserably as a slave. As he tossed these matters over in his mind, he became increasingly anxious and frightened, so that he could barely sleep. Finally, in a state of total exhaustion he submitted to God's will. And at that moment God prompted him to delay his journey to Ireland and go instead to Gaul in order to train as a preacher. There he learnt Latin, the only western language into which the Bible had been translated; and he studied the Bible in depth, learning the sayings and stories of Christ by heart. He also became familiar with the Christian doctrines which had been formulated since the time of Christ, and with the disputes which surrounded most of them. And he probably received some training in the art of rhetoric, although his autobiography does not mention or imply this. Only then did he feel ready to embark on his missionary venture.

The five preachers compared the training which they had received. Two of them had spent three years at a residential theological college. Two had done non-residential courses, reading and writing essays under the guidance of a tutor, and attending summer schools. The young woman had simply read the books recommended by Tom Birt, and discussed their contents with him. All of them had acquired a detailed knowledge of the Bible, and had become familiar with the various modern arguments as to how it should be interpreted. And all of them had learnt about Christian doctrine, and about the continuing disputes – virtually the same disputes which Patrick would have learnt about, and which still remain unresolved.

'Yet in all the years I've been preaching,' said the male vicar, 'I've never once referred to those doctrines – and nor do I ever refer to the arguments about biblical interpretation.' 'But in learning about all that,' the female vicar replied, 'it forced us to reflect on our faith, and work out for ourselves just what it means.' The man from central Kimford agreed with her, but pointed to the glaring gap in the training which most clergy receive: 'Unlike Patrick, we are not taught the art of rhetoric – the actual techniques of preaching. No wonder the standard of preaching in most churches is so abysmal.'

This led to a heated debate as to whether good preachers are born or taught. The man from central Kimford at first argued that preaching can be taught, and he summarized the techniques which aspiring preachers should learn. 'I learnt all that when I trained to be a teacher, before ordination,' said the male vicar, 'but lots of people who do the same training turn out to be bad teachers.' 'It's obviously a mixture of nature and nurture, like most things,' said the young woman. She added that Bishop Tom Birt was convinced that she had the gift of preaching, but all she knew was that she desperately needed training. 'Yes,' said the missioner, 'God bestows the gift, others test it and judge whether it's real – and then we go and get trained.'

'This may seem irrelevant,' interjected the female vicar, 'but, while we're talking about training, we ought to think about money. Regardless of whether it is good or bad, the Church of England spends a lot of money on training people for ministry. And almost all the money is spent on intellectual training – on educating people to be preachers and teachers. Yet under the new Celtic arrangement in Gyrwas Diocese, preaching is now only one ministry amongst six, all of equal importance. So how do we redress that balance?' 'Preachers need to be mentally bright and sharp,' responded the male vicar, 'but they don't need so much sheer knowledge as we were taught. The training could be much shorter, or less intense.' 'And surely it's wrong for those called to be pastors to receive this kind of education,' added the diocesan missioner. 'We need new kinds of courses to develop pastoral skills.' 'From now on,' the female vicar said, 'the training of preachers of Gyrwas Diocese is in our hands – the hands of this Order. So we can stipulate to theological colleges the length and extent of courses our preachers require. And we must ensure that money is left over for training other kinds of ministers.'

*   *   *   *   *

Patrick recognized both the power and the limitation of preaching. He could persuade people of the truth of the gospel, and strengthen the faith of those already converted. But he knew that people could only experience the gospel for themselves by becoming part of the vibrant and loving Christian community; and the existence of such communities was the living evidence for the truth proclaimed.

This meant that his early years in Ireland were extremely hard. There were virtually no Christians at all when he arrived, despite earlier missionary efforts by others, so there were no communities putting the gospel into practice. He thus concentrated on a small area, probably near the place where he had been a slave, converting a few people and forming a community. The joy which these first converts experienced through this spiritual fellowship began to attract others, so gradually the community grew. Patrick restrained his urge to move onwards, and instead devoted himself to nurturing this first church, training people in the various forms of ministry. Finally, when he felt confident that it could survive and flourish without him, he travelled to another part of the country. But this time he was not alone; he took with him a group from the church, so that in the new place he had a Christian community from the start which others could join. As a result the second church developed more rapidly, and he was able to undertake his next journey within a few months. And by this patient process of sowing and reaping he eventually covered the entire country.

At an early stage Patrick persuaded a chieftain in Armagh to give him some land; and there he established a college for the training of preachers. Thus in every new church he picked out the men who seemed most eloquent and fervent in their faith, and sent them to Armagh. Once they had finished their theological education, some joined Patrick on his journeys, helping him to preach the gospel in each new area. Most returned home to exercise their ministry in their own neighbourhood. But Patrick was insistent that preachers should not confine themselves to a single church. Instead he required them to move week by week and month by month from one church to another. In this way churches would hear the gospel presented in different ways, keeping the faith fresh. Patrick also told his preachers to listen to the congregations, as well as to speak, in order to learn their insights and ideas; the preachers could then convey these between churches, so that all could benefit.

The diocesan missioner observed that, despite the gospel having been preached in Gyrwas for at least thirteen centuries, many people are now almost as ignorant of the Christian faith as the Irish were when Patrick arrived; and in some of the poor areas of Gyrwas's cities and towns there is no Christian community. He pointed to three examples where flourishing churches had 'planted' groups of Christians in such areas – without realizing that they were imitating Patrick. 'But that's the exception, not the rule,' the man from central Kimford retorted. 'Most places have churches, but the preaching is so dull that fewer and fewer people go to them.' And he added that since resigning as vicar, he had received a steady stream of invitations to preach around the diocese and beyond – 'So I'm already one of Patrick's peripatetic preachers.'

'The problem is,' the diocesan missioner said, 'how we shift from the traditional system, in which the vicar preaches every week, to Patrick's system.' 'I don't think that's quite the right way of putting it,' said the young woman, 'because the new Celtic arrangements in Gyrwas already stipulate that, in the near future, only members of the Order will be allowed to preach. The problem is whether we can provide enough preachers to ensure that churches still have sermons.' 'And that depends on how stringent we are in selection,' added the female vicar. 'In my view,' said the Kimford preacher, 'it is better to have no sermon at all, rather than a bad one. So we should be very stringent, only admitting those who manifestly possess the gift of preaching.' 'I agree,' said the young woman. 'I'm fed up with bad sermons. And I don't think stringent selection will put people off from applying. As we said before, genuine preachers are as impelled to pursue their vocation as Patrick was.'

*　*　*　*　*

Patrick wrote his autobiography, not in order to tell the world of his extraordinary achievements, but as a defence against accusations of corruption. A group of church leaders, all of whom Patrick had converted, baptized and ordained, began to envy the great status he had acquired throughout Ireland; and they were also jealous of the precious gifts which wealthy people were bestowing on him.

So they charged him with using his ability as a preacher to persuade people to give him money, and with keeping this money for his own use. Patrick defended himself by saying, 'I have never asked even the price of a shoe as reward; and I have spent whatever money I have been given for the benefit of the poor.'

To the astonishment of the others, the diocesan missioner confessed that in the past he had been guilty of the charges levelled at Patrick: 'Although I never ask for money, my preaching induces many people to give lavishly to the charitable trust which pays my salary. And the trustees – all of whom are quite wealthy themselves – once used part of the money to raise my salary to almost twice the level of the ordinary parish clergy, as well as paying very generous travel expenses. For a few years I believed that I deserved this income as a reward for my ability and hard work – after all, I argued to myself, other people get paid according to ability and effort. And my high salary enabled me to send my son to an expensive school. But then he was expelled from the school for drug-taking. At first I was furious with the boy for having betrayed the good name of the family – and terrified that my own reputation would be damaged. Then when I remembered that I had taken drugs at the same age, I was filled with remorse; and I took the incident as a judgement on myself. I immediately asked the charitable trust to halve my salary – and my son went to the local state school, where he obtained excellent results.'

The diocesan missioner's honesty prompted the man from Kimford to confess his own moral anxieties as a preacher. 'Preaching,' he said, 'is the most public of Christian ministries; and inspiring preachers gain great respect and admiration from their congregations, and even personal adoration from more susceptible listeners. At the very least preachers, like actors and comedians, enjoy the buzz of having a favourable audience; and the ego of the preacher, like that of the actor and comedian, soon starts to inflate, all the more because most preachers, like actors and comedians, are quite vulnerable, insecure people. The difference is that actors and comedians are allowed, even expected, to have big

38

heads, while the Christian preacher should boast only in Christ. Keeping my ego under control is a constant battle; and, to be honest, I've lost hope of ever gaining a decisive victory.'

'Is it a mistake to have an Order of specialist preachers?' one of the vicars asked. 'Won't we just become a mutual admiration society, a bunch of clerical luvvies?' The young woman said she was beginning to feel quite scared of becoming a preacher: that being a preacher would isolate her from people, and make it even more difficult for her to make friends. The Kimford man replied that his recent experience was the reverse of what she feared. 'By resigning as vicar and declaring myself to be a preacher, I'm like a homosexual who has just come out – so people can now relate to the real me.' And he added that an Order of preachers is probably the best antidote – apart from a critical spouse – to the ballooning ego: 'It's the one context where we can be honest about the problem, just as we are being now.'

At the end of his autobiography, Patrick writes his creed, his summary of what he preached. There is nothing special or extraordinary in it. Or rather, as the young woman said, it is remarkable for its simplicity – 'It could almost have been written by children at Sunday School.' 'So did I waste my time at theological college?' one of the vicars asked. 'And did Patrick waste his time in Gaul?'

The group began to discuss the precise nature of the faith: what people are required to believe in order to be Christian. The conversation started quietly, but gradually rose in volume, turning into the most vigorous debate of all their sessions. Until then they had each been careful not to refer to their different theological positions, treating questions of churchmanship as forbidden territory; now, before they realized what they were doing, they had broken down the fences and marched on to it. The diocesan missioner held strict evangelical views, insisting that Christians should accept every word of the Bible as divinely-inspired. The Kimford man was more flexible on biblical authority, but shared the missioner's conviction that people must believe in the virgin birth and the bodily resurrection of Christ in order to be saved, believing that all who are aware of the Christian message, but do not accept it, exclude themselves from salvation. The male vicar, who belonged to the 'catholic' wing of the Church of England, also insisted that clear and firm doctrines are important, but expressed unease at the fierce language which evangelicals sometimes use. The female vicar was proudly liberal on matters of doctrine, saying that creeds and doctrinal formulae are no more than signposts, erected by fallible human beings, pointing to divine truths which are beyond words; the only question being whether the signposts are helpful or unhelpful.

After three-quarters of an hour, the young woman, who had remained quiet, interjected: 'Nothing of what any of you has said could be understood by a child, even the most intelligent and precocious child imaginable.' There was silence: the obvious remark felt to all of them like a severe reprimand. Then they began to defend themselves, saying that they were compelled to engage in these debates because of the ways in which the Christian faith had been distorted and corrupted over the centuries. 'Yes, exactly,' she said, 'it's human beings that make Christianity so complicated, but the gospel itself is very simple – and it's only by keeping it simple that we can enjoy even a fraction of Patrick's success.' The diocesan missioner continued to defend himself, saying that many people had come forward at his rallies in response to the strong, uncompromising message he delivered. 'Yes, and think of the 98 per cent of the population that would never come near your rallies,' she retorted.

The high-church vicar, who was well-versed in the history of the early Church, observed that almost every doctrine had been formulated as a result of a dispute; and, since preachers must always be ready to answer people's queries and questions, they need to reflect deeply on doctrinal matters. 'And this points to a paradox in the art of preaching,' he continued. 'On the one hand our sermons should be very simple, even child-like, because the gospel is simple; but on the other hand we must be complicated, because people's responses are often complicated.' 'That's why Jesus often used stories, and never used doctrinal formulae,' the liberal vicar replied. 'Stories are simple and complex at the same time.'

The five of them acknowledged that on the complicated aspects of preaching – the doctrinal arguments – they could sit together for fifty years, and still not agree. But on the simple aspects – the gospel itself – they recognized that their message was basically the same; and for that reason they could be members of a single Order of preachers.

*   *   *   *   *

In September 2003 Tom Birt asked the five preachers whether they were ready to extend the Order of St Patrick, to include all in Gyrwas Diocese whom God was calling to the preaching ministry. The diocesan missioner and the Kimford preacher were positive, without qualification. The two vicars also replied positively, but said that they believed they also possessed pastoral gifts, and thought that a significant number of other clergy probably also regarded themselves as both pastors and preachers. They thus asked for assurance that people could belong to both the Order of St Cuthbert and the Order of St Patrick. Tom Birt replied that the Celtic model put no limits on the number of Orders a person could join: 'It depends entirely on how God spreads his gifts – and on the judgement of the parishes and the Orders themselves.' The young woman said that she wanted to resign her membership of the Order, and apply afresh as a probationary member, in the hope of being trained properly. Tom Birt was momentarily offended, since he had been training her personally; but he accepted her desire not to be treated as a special case.

The four remaining members wrote to all the parishes and all the clergy, and also the Readers, inviting them to apply for membership of the Order of St Patrick. They emphasized that the purpose of the Order was to raise greatly the quality of preaching. So they would come to listen to applicants, both clergy and Readers, who already preached regularly, and would receive immediately into membership only those whose sermons were of a high standard. Other applicants would be tested to see if they possessed the basic gift, and then would undergo training.

Tom Birt also wrote to the clergy, Readers and parishes, urging them to try to discern honestly the gift of preaching – actual or potential – in their midst. He reminded them that, once the Celtic scheme for Gyrwas Diocese had fully come into operation, only members of the Order of St Patrick would be allowed to preach; so at least a hundred people needed to join the Order if the churches in the diocese were to be properly served. All who were accepted into the Order would be ordained by him as preachers; and those who were not already clergy would also be trained and ordained as priests, allowing them, like the pastors, to preside at Communion services. He concluded by saying that parishes and preachers were free to make whatever financial arrangements they wished: preachers could be paid a regular salary; they could be paid per engagement; or they could take no remuneration. They were also free to support preachers to exercise their ministry elsewhere, both in poorer parishes and outside the church – and he urged richer parishes to consider this.

4. HEALERS

The Order of St Brigid

The Order of St Brigid was formed on 1 February, her traditional feast day, 2004. At the centre of Gyrwas Cathedral, where the north and south transepts meet under the tower, a small fire was lit at the start of the service. It recalled the fire which burnt continuously in the chapel of Brigid's monastery, and was kept alight for a thousand years until the Reformation, to symbolize the healing presence of God in our midst. In his sermon Tom Birt spoke of how Christ had sent out his disciples both to preach the gospel and to heal the sick. 'Sermons are preached week by week in churches throughout the Christian world,' Tom Birt said, 'and here in Gyrwas we are taking practical steps to improve their quality. But we seem to have forgotten the ministry of healing.' He described how in ancient Ireland Patrick, the great preacher, and Brigid, the great healer, were seen as the father and mother of the Church; their two ministries were seen as complementary, each depending on the other. 'Indeed healing – making people whole – fulfils the gospel; it is the words of the gospel put into practice.'

Tom Birt invited five people, with quite varied knowledge and experience of healing, to be the founding members. The first had been holding monthly healing services for the past decade in a village church near Kimford, where her husband was vicar. The services, which were emotionally highly charged, now attracted many hundreds of people; and the regular attenders claimed that numerous miracles had occurred. The second was a doctor in general practice in Kimford itself; she was a long-standing member of a church in the centre of the city which was renowned for its liberal and open-minded approach to religion. The third was the vicar of a church in an old industrial city in the north-west of Gyrwas diocese, and he too held monthly healing services. He belonged to the catholic wing of the church; and at the climax of his services he invited all who wished for healing – either for themselves or for someone else – to come and kneel at the altar, where he and another priest laid hands on their heads. He also visited many sick people in their homes and in hospitals, and anointed their foreheads with oil. The fourth was the warden of a large old house in the far west of the diocese, where groups came for conferences and retreats. The fifth was a psychotherapist who had her own practice, and also took referrals from the local doctors.

The five met each fortnight to reflect on the ministry of healing, in the light of both their own experience and the example of Brigid.

*   *   *   *   *

More than that of any other Celtic saint, the life of Brigid is shrouded in legend and fantasy. The five healers quickly decided that they would not even try to distinguish historical truth from myth, but instead look at whatever episodes and stories contained lessons and insights.

She was the daughter of a wealthy Irish chieftain. She grew up at the time Patrick was preaching the gospel, but he had not yet reached her part of the country. Nevertheless she possessed a natural generosity, and frequently raided the huge larder in her father's castle in order to give food to the poor and needy living nearby. This made her father furious, and eventually he decided to sell her as a slave to another chieftain, so he grabbed her, threw her in the back of his chariot, and they travelled a long distance to the other castle. Her father went in to negotiate a price. But as a sign of respect he entered the castle unarmed, leaving his royal sword, with its handle encrusted with jewels, in the chariot with Brigid. In the meantime a leper passed by, and begged Brigid for food. 'I have no food,' she replied, 'in fact, I feel hungry myself. But take the sword, sell it, and then buy food.'

When her father emerged from the castle, having agreed a price for Brigid, and saw what she had done, his fury knew no bounds, and he began to beat her with his belt. The other chieftain, realizing that he too would become a victim of Brigid's generosity if he

44

accepted her, declared that he had changed his mind. So Brigid
was spared from slavery by the warmth of her spirit.

'The moral of the story, that generosity brings its own reward,' said the doctor, 'is not its real message. Brigid's generosity was not the result of religious or moral teaching, and so was not an act of will. Rather, it flowed easily and naturally. She reached out to others by instinct and inclination. I'm not sure whether I'm a real healer, or just a mechanic of the body. But I do know that Brigid's natural generosity is the main characteristic of a healer.' 'Yes,' agreed the retreat house warden, 'the healer must want nothing in return for what is given – not even moral satisfaction – because any kind of self-interest is a barrier to the healing process.'

Both the woman and the vicar who held monthly healing services spoke of how they spent a long period in prayer immediately prior to the services. They did not pray for the people who needed healing, nor did they ask God for strength and grace. Instead they simply emptied themselves of all thought and feeling, so that by the time of the service they had no wishes or even hopes about what would happen. 'Only then can I truly be a channel of God's healing love,' the woman said.

The psychotherapist spoke of the importance of the ten-minute break she took between clients. After she had dictated notes on the previous appointment into a tape recorder, she sat in silence, relaxing both her body and her mind. She also spoke of the need to monitor her own emotions constantly during the sessions. 'I may feel anger, irritation, warmth, even sexual attraction; and these feelings often tell me something important about the client. But if I allow my feelings to influence my words or even my bodily movements, I can do terrible damage. Only by taking control of them and overcoming them can I help the client.'

The doctor said that her colleagues in the practice would throw her out if she took a ten-minute break between patients. 'And,' she added 'there are days when irritation with my patients overwhelms me – all their self-pitying grumbles and whinges.' She admitted that much of her work was mechanical, and could be done equally well by a computer: the patient's symptoms could be typed in, and the appropriate treatment printed out. 'Yet I know that most patients don't want a machine. They want me, for the brief period when they are in my surgery, to concentrate wholly on them, to the exclusion of all else. And that is as much part of the healing process as the medicines I hand out.'

* * * * *

Brigid eventually ran away from home. She had heard about Patrick, and went to the part of Ireland where he was staying, to hear him preach. She was captivated with what she heard, and immediately asked him to prepare her for baptism. He recognized her special qualities, and after he had baptized her, suggested that she start a community, dedicated to hospitality and healing. She returned to her home territory in the east of Ireland and built herself a hut under a large oak tree. Soon others, both men and women, came to join her, and it became the largest settlement in the whole country.

Brigid called the community Cill Dara, *meaning Cell of the Oak, which was later anglicized to Kildare. But it was called by others 'The City of the Poor and the Sick'. Families brought sick relatives to be nursed by the members of the community; and the community also welcomed those suffering from mental sickness. Brigid herself led a group of women each night to tour the local paths and roads, inviting those who were sleeping rough to come back to the community for food and shelter. No one was ever turned away.*

The warden of the retreat house in west Gyrwas sighed: 'If only we could be as open-handed and open-hearted . . .' He described their attempts to include mentally sick people as part of the residential group; but even one person with schizophrenia could cause intolerable tensions and divisions, so that the group barely had any energy left to look after guests. And when they started welcoming tramps and wayfarers, they often had no space for paying guests, and so the income of the house began to plummet. 'Yet I know

46

that hospitality is an essential part of Christian discipleship,' the warden concluded, 'and by welcoming people as we find them, we affirm and uplift them.'

The vicar related his experience as a young man, when he and his girlfriend were back-packing in Australia, being taken in by a small community of nuns. 'The prioress said to us that God had brought us into their midst, and we were welcome to stay as long as we wished. I replied that neither of us believed in God; and besides, we were not married, so our presence would cause them scandal. The prioress laughed, saying that God would soon sort out our beliefs; and when he had done that, he might arrange a wedding as well. Being accepted as we were, without any demand being made of us, was the first stage in my conversion – and in my girlfriend's conversion. And we've now been married thirty-four years.'

There was silence. Then the doctor turned to the warden of the retreat house. 'You do your share of hospitality already, welcoming all those groups; you shouldn't try to do more.' She said that most evenings she was too exhausted to do anything but flop down in front of the television; and that she found having people to stay overnight in her house very intrusive and stressful. Yet she recognized that to invite someone into one's own home can be a great blessing, both for oneself and for the guest. So on her day off she tried always to ask one or two people in her village for coffee, especially those who seemed lonely or had been recently bereaved. 'I just hope they don't feel I'm taking pity on them,' she laughed.

'So what's this all got to do with healing?' the woman who took monthly healing services asked. The doctor answered that healing services and anointing people with oil are the external, visible aspects of the healing process – rather like the drugs she prescribes. 'But any doctor and nurse will tell you that people only get better if they are in the right frame of mind – if their soul is right, to use the religious term. Accepting people as they are, loving them as God made them, helps to put the soul in order.' The vicar added that he regarded his healing services as the tip of the iceberg; the main work of healing was done in the visits he made between the services.

'I know that our styles are very different,' the vicar said to the woman healer, 'but the reality is very similar. You have started a Fellowship of Healing; and the members of your Fellowship who live in my parish are constantly popping into each other's homes, and inviting others along as well – that's why the Fellowship grows so quickly. It's because of all that invisible activity that so many wonderful things happen at your services.' 'Yes,' she said quietly, 'I know that.' 'In that case,' said the psychotherapist, 'the Order of St Brigid shouldn't just include specialists and professionals like us. It should include everyone who makes a point of being hospitable – who can welcome and love people, without making demands on them.'

*   *   *   *   *

Brigid ordered the men in her community to clear a large area of land for cultivation; and then they grew the largest and sweetest fruits and vegetables in the whole of Ireland. Next she arranged for a large kitchen to be built, so that the food could be prepared to the highest standards, insisting that every member and guest should eat and drink well. But she would not allow any meat to be eaten. On the contrary, she demanded that any animal that came into the community should be offered food, like a human guest; and injured animals should be nursed back to health.

The doctor confessed that she was a meat-eater, but none the less she admired Brigid's attitude to the natural world, enjoying to the full its bounty, and yet also respecting its integrity. The vicar urged the group to shift its focus from healing to wholeness: 'The purpose of healing is to make people whole – in fact the two words "healing" and "wholeness" have the same root. Brigid understood that wholeness in nature and wholeness of the individual are closely linked. We can only be made whole within ourselves if our relationship with the natural order is also made whole.' The woman healer reacted with nervous aggression, saying that such ideas sounded distinctly pagan.

48

'All right,' said the psychotherapist, 'what do we think Jesus meant when he spoke about people being made whole?' The doctor replied that Hippocrates, the founder of western medicine four hundred years before Christ, taught that physical illness is caused by the different parts of the body working in disharmony; and thus making people well means bringing the different parts back into harmony. 'Jesus applied the same principle to the human spirit,' she added, 'and he also saw the close link between spiritual wholeness and physical wholeness – when the spirit is made whole, the body's own healing forces are released.'

'That is why love and wholeness are so closely linked,' the psychotherapist said. 'In fact, I think they mean the same thing. My job is to help people understand and love themselves, the whole of themselves, the nasty bits as well as the nice bits; and I do that by trying to love and understand them myself, without wanting them to be different. Once they can love themselves as a whole, then they can get all the different bits to work together.' 'And when that happens,' the doctor added, 'many of their physical problems get better as well.'

* * * * *

To the west of Kildare the land was owned by a man who was persistently hostile to the Christian faith. And he was extremely cruel to the families who lived and worked on his land, taking for himself such a large portion of their harvest that they were constantly hungry, and punishing severely even minor misdemeanours. The whole region lived in fear of his anger. Brigid and her community prayed daily for his tenants, that they might be set free from their misery; and they also prayed for him, that he might be set free from the evil spirit that ruled his life.

Every few months Brigid walked over to his castle in the hope of persuading him to change his ways; and he always ordered his servants to chase her away. One day Brigid heard that this harsh man had been taken seriously ill. Brigid immediately went to his castle, and on this occasion he let her in, allowing her to come to his bedside. Although he would not greet her, she sensed that he was pleased to see her. She told him that he was his own worst

victim, that his cruel heart had made him miserable. And she
promised him that if, even at this late stage, he turned away from
evil and sought love, he could enjoy inner peace and joy. He made
no reply, and she left. She returned a week later, by which time
he had grown weaker; she said the same thing, and again he did
not reply.

For several weeks Brigid continued to visit him without success,
as his physical condition worsened. Then on the final occasion she
found that he was too weak to speak. She decided that she would
remain silent also, and communicate by signs. She leant down and
picked up some of the straw used to cover the floor, and tied it into
the shape of a cross. She held the cross in front of him, and he
nodded. He slowly raised his right arm, and pointed to a bowl of
water in the corner of the room. Brigid brought the bowl of water
to his bed, and baptized him. For the first time in his life a smile
of happiness came over his face; and a few moments later he died.

The vicar said that care for the dying is the most important
of the healing ministry. 'All of us will eventually die, and
death is the moment when, through God's grace, we can
be made fully whole. That is what Christ's resurrection is
all about.' 'I agree with you,' replied the doctor, 'but not
many of my patients do. They come to me in order to get
well; and if I can't make them well, they think I've failed.'

The woman healer began to speak, then stopped. The
others pressed her to continue; and after a pause she said
that she wanted to share a profound anxiety about her own
ministry, an anxiety she had never expressed openly before.
She described at length the kind of people that attended
her services, some with minor physical ailments, some with
mental problems, and some with very serious illnesses that
might be terminal. 'Despite great faith the seriously ill
people often do not get better. Happily many of them, even
as life slips away, are able to thank me for the comfort I've
given them. But a few feel horribly guilty, believing that
their own wickedness is preventing miracles from occurring;
and they may die convinced that they are eternally
damned.'

The doctor, who privately disapproved of the woman's
methods, wanted to say, 'Well, at least their relatives don't

sue you.' But she was so moved by the woman's candour that she held her tongue. The psychotherapist broke the silence. 'We may seem very different, but you and I are in the same trade. I don't even pretend to mend people's bodies, and the truth is that you don't mend their bodies either. Both of us are mending their minds, their emotions, their souls. In some cases healing the soul also causes the body to get better. When that happens in your services, it's called a divine miracle; when it happens in my consulting room, God isn't usually mentioned. And, of course, the most important time to heal the soul is when the body is dying; after all, everyone wants to die in peace.'

The warden of the retreat house asked if the discussion could be brought back to the ordinary parish. He said that, as the years had passed, he had realized that his own ministry was very similar to those people in parishes who, without any fuss or ceremony, consistently visit their sick neighbours, to bring a hot meal and have a chat – 'the only difference being that they visit the sick, whereas in my case the sick visit me.' He reckoned that over half the people who stayed at his retreat house had some kind of illness or were in some form of distress, and were seeking relief. He and other members of the retreat house could offer nothing more than good food and gentle conversation; and yet astonishingly people went away full of gratitude and praise. 'What we're doing in our rather feeble way is what Brigid did for that landowner. But more importantly, that's what the unsung good neighbours in every parish of the land are doing. And when death approaches, that quiet ministry eases the journey from this world to the next.'

'We've come back in a great circle to where we were a few weeks ago,' the psychotherapist observed. She reminded them that at the end of a previous session they had decided that the Order of St Brigid should include everyone who makes a point of being hospitable, inviting people into their homes. Now they wanted to include everyone who made a point of visiting people in their own homes. 'Yes,' said the vicar, 'the healing ministry is a kind of reaching out ministry, just as Jesus reached out to those who

51

were sick and touched them.' 'At this rate,' concluded the doctor, 'our Order will be bigger than all the others put together – which is probably right.'

* * * * *

In July 2004 Tom Birt came to visit a session of the group, and asked them if they were ready to extend the Order of St Brigid. They replied that in their view the Order should be open, including all those who bring comfort and encouragement to others. And they felt that any kind of selection process, testing people's gift, would be not only invidious but also impossible, since by its nature the healing ministry is largely hidden. The main purpose of the Order would simply be to enable people to support one another by meeting in groups from time to time – 'just as the five original members, by common consent, had received wonderful support from one another in the previous five months. 'So you don't think any training is necessary for the healing ministry?' Tom Birt asked. They answered that the best training is experience – and then opportunity to share this experience, and the insights gained from it, with others.

The vicar now raised an anxiety: that many of the people who exercise a healing ministry do not recognize it as such; and besides, most of them are quiet and diffident people who would be reluctant to join an Order for healers. Tom Birt responded that, in addition to providing a context for mutual support, the purpose of the Order was to raise the status and importance of the healing ministry in people's minds. Thus the very existence of the Order would affirm the work of those who did not wish to join. The warden of the retreat house suggested that they should aim to get at least one person in each parish or group of parishes to join the Order. That person could be seen as a local leader or representative, and in due course could be encouraged to convene informal meetings of others in the parish who share the ministry.

Tom Birt then asked about money: Should healers receive money for their work? The psychotherapist said that the payment of money by her clients, in addition to providing her with a livelihood, also assisted the work itself: it made the clients use the time with her well. The woman healer replied that, since Christian healing is based on selfless generosity, there should be no direct material reward. The psychotherapist bridled at this apparent judgement on her work, and added, 'Money is not simply a reward, it is also a symbol. If my clients didn't pay me, they would feel they were in my debt, and their self-respect and sense of personal freedom would be compromised.' The vicar intervened, saying that, of all the six ministries which Gyrwas diocese was formally authorizing, healing was the most private and personal. Thus individuals must be left to judge for themselves as to whether payment should form part of the healing relationship; the Order should remain silent on the matter.

Tom Birt then brought the discussion back to the question of membership. He understood why the Order itself could not select its members, but said that there must be some means of testing people's gift. As a matter of principle the discernment of a spiritual gift must be shared by the individual and by representatives of the Christian community. And without any testing, an Order of healers could easily attract every kind of crank and charlatan. The warden of the retreat centre replied that, since healing was such a personal and private ministry, the only people in a position to judge someone's gift are those who know that person well, and can observe the quality of his or her relationships with others. Thus local congregations should be encouraged to discern and affirm those in their midst who exercise a healing ministry. The vicar said that in practice it would be very difficult for an entire congregation to make such a judgement; and a congregation could not draw out the healing gifts that are latent. He thus proposed that the pastors should nominate people to be members of the Order of St Brigid. And the pastors might also help those with a healing gift to overcome their diffidence about it, thus allowing their ministry to be affirmed.

Thus the five founding members of the Order of St Brigid wrote a letter to all the members of the Order of St Cuthbert, asking them to propose names. They described the healing ministry, as they had come to understand it, emphasizing hospitality and neighbourhood visiting, as well as its more visible and public forms. And they also outlined the purposes of the Order, as a context for mutual support, and as a means of raising the profile of this vital aspect of Christian work. After sending the letter they decided that a similar letter should be sent every year, to tell new pastors and remind old pastors that nurturing the healing ministry in their congregations is a vital part of their own ministry.

5. ARTISTS

The Order of St Columba

The Order of St Columba was formed on 9 June, the saint's traditional feast day, 2005. In his sermon at the inaugural service Tom Birt spoke of the artistic genius which surrounds Christian worship – and which Christians too easily take for granted. There are the ancient parish churches in which Christians meet, of which Gyrwas Diocese alone boasts about four hundred; these buildings embody the creativity of countless generations of craftsmen, going right back to Norman times and beyond, each adding something new and fresh to what was already there. There are the wonderful hymns which Christians sing, in which profound poetry is married to sublime melodies. There are the prayers which Christians recite, in which majestic human language penetrates the mysteries of God's truth. Yet Christian worship should not merely relish the genius of the past, or else it will become stale and dull. The present generation must nurture the creative impulse in its own bosom, and find its own way of responding to God's glory.

Then Tom Birt posed a question to the congregation assembled in Gyrwas Cathedral, itself a building of breathtaking beauty. Is artistic activity the preserve of a small élite, a tiny minority who are in some way quite different from the rest of us, or are artistic gifts more widely spread? Certainly very few can write poetry to match the works of Charles Wesley and George Herbert which appear in our hymnbooks; God does not give many the gift to compose melodies like Jerusalem and Crimond. Carving even the most simple gargoyle is far beyond the skill of most of us. Yet what about the choirs and musicians who interpret the hymns and melodies? And why is the Church today so bereft of painters and sculptors, when the Church in earlier times was so rich in such artists? Could it be that many people's latent artistic gifts are being wasted?

Tom Birt concluded his sermon with a further, more difficult question: Are artists the people who break down the invisible walls which divide the Church from the wider community? In the Celtic period, and right up until relatively recent times, all art was religious; and there was no division in people's minds between the religious and secular aspects of their lives – all life was permeated by religion. Now those who hold a clear religious faith are in a minority, and religion is widely perceived as a separate sphere of activity, a kind of hobby which this minority pursues in their leisure hours. Yet artistic creativity knows no barriers: artists draw their inspiration from every kind of source, making no distinction between religion and the rest of life; and good music, poetry, painting, architecture and sculpture can be appreciated by everybody, regardless of religious affiliation – or lack of it. So just as the Order of St Brigid is concerned with the healing of individuals, the Order of St Columba may have a particular role in the healing of society.

As with the other Orders, Tom Birt invited five people to be founder members of the Order of St Columba. The first was the organist and choirmaster of a small village church in the north-west of Gyrwas, who had composed modern settings to the traditional Anglican canticles. The second was a painter with a studio in Kimford, who made his living painting family portraits, but had also painted a triptych for one of the side altars of Gyrwas cathedral, and the stations of the cross for a parish church in a village near Kimford. The third was vicar of a wealthy suburb on the edge of Kimford, who had commissioned new sculptures and stained glass for his church, and who regularly organized exhibitions at the back of the nave for local artists. The fourth was a presenter on BBC Radio Gyrwas, who was also a churchwarden. And the fifth an architect with responsibility for over fifty churches in the diocese.

After hearing Tom Birt's sermon, all five of them wondered if the Order of St Columba should exist at all. As one of them said to Tom Birt over a cup of tea after the service,

'If artistic inspiration knows no barriers, why form an Order for artists within the Church?' Tom Birt replied that they should tackle that question; and if they concluded that an Order for artists should not exist, he would disband it. So the group began to meet each fortnight.

* * * * *

Columba was born in 521 in Donegal, the northernmost county of Ireland. His mother was of royal descent, and also a devout Christian. She employed a priest to teach him to read and write, and also to nurture his faith; she then sent him away to a man in the west of Ireland, renowned for the beauty of the hymns he composed and sang. Under the Druids, before the arrival of Christianity, bards had wandered from village to village, entertaining the people with religious ballads. Far from trying to abolish this practice, Patrick decided to adapt it for his purposes, urging the bards whom he converted to compose and sing Christian ballads, and he instituted an Order of bards ordained to this ministry. Columba's teacher was one of the leading Christian bards of his time, and inspired Columba to compose his own hymns. Soon Columba himself became an official bard, travelling from church to church. Judging by the handful of his hymns which survive, he had a remarkable gift for using images from nature to express spiritual experiences.

The choirmaster wondered whether Columba and the other Irish bards gave a performance at the churches they visited, like a soloist or a choir singing an anthem, or whether they encouraged congregational singing. The radio presenter replied that the bards probably did a mixture of the two: they performed their Christian ballads; but if the words and tunes were easy to pick up, people would continue to sing them after the bards had left. The painter said he had always thought of hymns as spiritual folk music, composed in such a way that people can easily learn and remember them – 'and it's good to think that Christian folk music goes right back to Columba's time.' 'Yes,' responded the architect, 'it's surprising how often a line or a verse from a hymn pops into my head, even in the most unexpected situations, such as when I'm up a ladder inspecting a roof.'

'That raises another question in my mind,' the choir-master said. He pointed out that Charles Wesley, the most prolific of English hymn-writers, went into taverns to listen to the popular songs, and then wrote Christian words to their tunes. And, although most hymn-writers since Wesley had not gone quite as far, they had generally used the popular musical idioms of their day. He suggested that most modern hymn tunes 'are post-Elvis Presley rock', and proceeded to sing his own spoof example, a few verses of John's Gospel to the Beatles' tune 'Yesterday', to illustrate his point. 'The question,' he concluded, 'is whether popular Christian music must always be derivative, copying and adapting secular music, or whether there can be specifically Christian styles of composition.'

'I think that's the wrong question to ask,' the vicar replied. Any attempt, he said, to develop special Christian types of music, or indeed any other form of art, is extremely dangerous, since it would make the cultural walls around Christianity even more impregnable. 'The purpose of the Christian faith,' he asserted, 'is to sanctify life in all its aspects – and that includes art. So Christian music should use all the techniques and idioms at its disposal, and in that sense be indistinguishable from secular music. The difference should lie in its inner spirit, which should be holy and divine. The question is whether our hymns contain the divine spirit; and I'm not sure that many of them do.'

'That sounds horribly snobby,' said the radio presenter. He suggested that Christmas carols should be regarded as models of Christian music: they tell a good story in a vivid way; they have great tunes which everyone can hum; and professional recordings of carols slot comfortably alongside modern pop songs in December radio programmes. 'If only we could have equally good Christian songs for other times of the year, then we'd be getting somewhere.'

The architect suggested that the vicar and the radio presenter were making the same point in different ways. They both seemed to agree that Christian music should not try to be special or different, but simply be as good as possible. Thus the challenge for Christian composers and singers is to express the gospel in words and music which people want to hear – and then to sing. 'Does that mean that all Christian music must be pop music?' asked the choirmaster plaintively. 'It should be whatever people like,' the architect replied, 'and happily, in God's rich and varied world, different people have different tastes. So long as people want your canticles and anthems, you can go on composing and singing them.'

*   *   *   *   *

The monastic communities which Patrick, Brigid and their immediate successors had formed were devoted almost entirely to prayer and hospitality. Columba, however, looked back to the earlier Druid communities of priests, which were great centres of culture and education, attracting artists, scholars and pupils from Britain and the rest of Europe, as well as from Ireland itself. He conceived the idea of founding a network of Christian monasteries across Ireland, which would combine prayer and hospitality with scholastic and artistic endeavour. He fulfilled only a small part of this grand ambition, creating communities at Derry, Durrow and Kells, before he found himself on the losing side of a major political conflict, and was forced to flee to Scotland. But the monastery he founded at Iona, and those which his followers founded elsewhere, including Aidan's monastery at Lindisfarne, spread his vision right across the British Isles.

The most famous product of these Columban monasteries is the Book of Kells, *which in fact may have been made at Lindisfarne, about a century after Aidan's death. But numerous other works of art survive, including silver and wooden boxes to carry relics, richly decorated stone crosses, and other illuminated manuscripts. The Celtic artists drew inspiration from manuscripts which found their way to the British Isles from Egypt and Syria, and they also adopted patterns and motifs from Druid sources. The schools which they ran played a major role in instilling Christian values in Irish and British society.*

The Kimford painter sighed with envy. 'I would love to devote myself entirely to religious art, and be free of these wretched portraits I have to churn out.' The choirmaster wondered whether communities of artists could be formed again. 'Nobody would buy their work,' the painter replied, 'so they would be communities of starvation.' The radio presenter added that artists are too individualist nowadays to be held together in a community. 'Those calligraphers who did the *Book of Kells* worked under a strict discipline, with strict rules and traditions governing the forms and colours – just like icon painters in Russia and Greece. Modern artists in the west like to do what they want.'

The vicar agreed with the painter from Kimford that the market for religious art 'has dwindled to a tiny trickle – though occasionally I try to pump it up again'. But he said that the group was missing the crucial elements in the Columban communities. Firstly, the monks were not trying to sell their art; they were doing it for the glory of God, and it was received in that spirit. In other words, the monastic artists were not professionals, in the sense that they depended on their art for their livelihood; they spent much of the day on the land growing food for themselves. Secondly, they were not engaged in religious art, as distinct from other forms of art. On the contrary, the genius of the Celtic artists lay in their ability to relate spiritual themes with natural images. 'So I try to encourage the amateur artist – "amateur" in the proper sense, meaning that they work for the love of it. And in the exhibitions I hold in my church, I make no stipulations about the kind of paintings and sculptures which are displayed. All good art is spiritual – it reflects and expresses the depths of the human spirit.'

'So where do the likes of me fit in?' the Kimford painter asked. 'I work for love, but I need bread as well.' The vicar replied that in practice there was a distinction between the small number of full-time artists, and the much larger number of people who have the potential to create things of beauty in their spare time. The full-timers are needed for the major permanent features in our churches, such as stained-glass windows, altar vessels, furniture and memorials. But the real challenge is to harness the gifts of others to create more ephemeral pieces. 'By the time the *Book of Kells* was made,' he continued, 'people were beginning to paint the walls of their church with pictures illustrating the gospel stories and the lives of the saints. And inevitably these paintings only last a few years – just think of your decorating at home. So there was limitless opportunity for local artists to exercise their gifts, and for others to be uplifted by what they did. Wouldn't it be wonderful if our churches came alive again with the art of local people?'

The choirmaster was not so sure, suggesting that most British people nowadays prefer their churches plain and simple. 'Besides,' he asked, 'how does that fit in with your notion that anything goes? I doubt if people would like an erotic nude hanging next to the altar.' The vicar agreed that his earlier remarks were too extreme. 'I can get away with the occasional nude tucked away at the back of the nave. But I know that if paintings and sculptures were to spread eastward up the church, the subject matter would have to be more clearly religious.' The architect went back to the vicar's statement that all art is spiritual. 'It's true that good art reflects the human spirit, but that doesn't mean that good art always glorifies God – because the human spirit doesn't always glorify God. An icon painter is supposed to be in the right spiritual state when he starts his work. And the spiritual devotion of those Columban monasteries was the soil in which their wonderful works of art grew.'

'That's the point of the Order of St Columba,' interjected the radio presenter. 'The purpose is not to provide art classes – people can learn the necessary skills elsewhere. It's to draw out and affirm people's artistic gifts, and then encourage them to use those gifts in the right spirit. I may be naïve, but I think if they knew they were doing something for the church, they'd actually want to glorify God. Church buildings for some reason evoke those feelings.' 'And I've found,' the vicar said with a smile, 'that when local people have contributed to the beauty of the church, they and their families and their friends are more likely to want to worship there.' 'That even happens for a few weeks after a flower festival, until the flowers fade,' added the choirmaster.

*   *   *   *   *

Although a few stone huts and oratories, built in the shape of beehives, survive, most Celtic churches consisted of two rectangular chambers: a large tall chamber where the congregation gathered; and at its east end a small chamber where the altar stood. The square east end remains to this day a distinctive feature of Irish and British churches; elsewhere the east end of churches is semi-circular, echoing the shape of a Roman basilica.

But to the Celtic eye it was not only the building which was holy; the site on which it stood was also holy. The places where Columba founded his monasteries had earlier been the sites of Druid temples and communities. Similarly when he and his followers preached the gospel in Britain, they urged the new Christians not to tear down their old pagan places of worship, but to adapt them for Christian worship. As a result most parish churches in the British Isles stand on ground which people have regarded as sacred for many thousands of years.

The vicar suggested that church architecture is the one form of high art that is almost universally popular; virtually the entire British population appreciates the beauty of a medieval village church. The radio presenter added that church buildings are the only aspect of formal, organized religion that continues to evoke deep spiritual feelings in people. 'Yes,' the vicar agreed, 'if I wanted to pull down my church and replace it with something more practical, those who never attend services would be even more outraged than those who do so.'

The architect asked why church buildings are so beautiful, and then proceeded to answer his own question. 'The first thing is that people want their church to be beautiful precisely because it's a sacred building on a sacred site; and when people want beauty, they usually find it. The second thing is that it embodies the community, and expresses its highest feelings. Every generation over the centuries has contributed something: built an aisle, raised the roof, extended the chancel, put in a new window, installed a pulpit or whatever. And somehow the spirit in which all these things has been done causes them to blend together in wonderful harmony. No single architect could create anything as remotely beautiful as a humble parish church.'

'So why do you people,' asked the radio presenter, 'want to conserve everything in aspic? Getting permission to make even the smallest change is the devil's own job. Our ancestors were allowed to make their mark, but we're not.' 'It's because most modern stuff is so ghastly,' interrupted the choirmaster. 'Yes,' agreed the architect, 'but then most modern stuff has always been ghastly. I suspect that the really horrid things which our ancestors did to the churches were demolished a few generations ago. So a kind of refining process went on. The point of our present rules and regulations is to prevent the horrid things happening in the first place. The danger is that we stifle good things.'

'To be honest,' said the vicar, 'I don't think many good ideas are coming forward, because the creative spirit is so low in our churches. That's why we need the Order – to nurture the artistic spirit. If we can make this Order work well, parishes will be full of new visions and schemes. Of course, lots will be bad, so they can be sifted out. But some will be as good as anything in the past.' 'And where's the money going to come from?' asked the painter. 'As we were saying earlier, everyone loves churches,' replied the vicar, 'and most people feel that their parish church belongs to them. So let them all feel that they can play a part in enhancing this beauty – then they'll all want to contribute.' 'It sounds wonderful,' said the choirmaster, 'too wonderful.'

*　*　*　*　*

Towards the end of his life, long after his exile from Ireland, Columba heard that the bishops and priests of the Irish church were about to meet, in order to abolish the Order of bards, who they felt lacked discipline and encouraged excessive exuberance in worship. Columba, who even as an old man loved exuberant worship, was appalled. He had been ordered never again to set foot on Irish soil. So he tied clods of Scottish soil to his shoes and sailed back to Ireland. He then walked to the place where the bishops and priests were gathered; and with great eloquence persuaded them to allow the Order of bards to continue. Part of his discourse was in the form of a song, composed for the occasion.

'Let's hope that one day we get accused of being too exuberant,' the radio presenter joked. 'Yes,' said the vicar, 'we'll know we're doing our job right when some future Bishop of Gyrwas tries to stamp on us.' But the choirmaster, who shared the Irish bishops' dislike of exuberance, asked, 'And who is this "we" who will form this Order of St Columba? We're a pretty motley bunch, with not much in common. Who do we invite to join us?'

In choosing them as the five founding members, Tom Birt had made clear that he wanted all the arts – music, architecture and even the broadcasting media, as well as painting and sculpture – to be included. And in their own discussions they had agreed that amateurs and professionals alike should be welcomed. 'But what about the likes of me?' the vicar asked. 'I have no artistic ability whatever. Yet I love the arts, and like to do everything I can to encourage them. Should I be excluded?' There was a pause. The painter replied, 'Artists have always needed patrons and supporters. They also need critics from time to time, to tell them what they're doing wrong.'

'In fact,' said the radio presenter, 'I think it's as important to have supporters in this Order as the artists themselves. There are lots of people with artistic gifts out there. What they need is for others to recognize their gifts and encourage them. This Order should provide a context for people to meet and discuss how best this artistic ministry can be nurtured and channelled.'

*　*　*　*　*

In November Tom Birt asked the five members whether they were ready to expand their Order. They replied that they were, but felt unsure how to set about it. After discussion with Tom Birt, they decided to hold a series of conferences on successive Saturdays in the following May and June. Each conference would be devoted to a particular art, discussing how it can enhance people's worship and spiritual experience. At the end they would invite participants to form a cell, to find ways of nurturing and encouraging that art within Gyrwas Diocese.

So the dates were fixed, and a letter of invitation sent to every parish. In the letter they said that the Order would be open to anyone who wished to join. The only requirement was that members should want to play a part in the artistic ministry of Gyrwas, either directly through exercising their own artistic gifts, or indirectly through supporting the artistic endeavours of others.

6. ADMINISTRATORS

The Order of St Iltut

The Order of St Iltut was founded on 6 November, the saint's traditional feast day, 2005. Alone among the six Orders formed in Gyrwas Diocese, this was to correspond precisely with an existing office in the Church of England, that of churchwarden. And all the churchwardens – two in every parish church – were invited to the inaugural service at Gyrwas Cathedral. However, following the same process as he had with the other Orders, Tom Birt chose five churchwardens as founding members, to discuss the nature and purpose of the Order in the light of the life and teaching of its patron saint. Then half a year later the Order would be expanded.

In his sermon at the inaugural service, Tom Birt spoke of the parish church as the first democratic institution in England, and the churchwarden as the first elected office. For over a millennium churchwardens have been chosen by the people whom they serve, and are directly accountable to them. Thus the office of churchwarden has kept alive the Celtic vision of the church, in which the people themselves discern and affirm one another's spiritual gift. And it is important, Tom Birt emphasized, to see the gift of administration, which is the churchwarden's distinctive role, as spiritual, akin to that of pastorship, preaching and the rest, and not merely as material. Admittedly the churchwarden's primary functions are to take care of the material assets of the parish, and to ensure that parish affairs are efficiently organized. But the way in which the churchwarden performs these tasks can to a great degree determine whether the Christian community is harmonious and generous, or quarrelsome and mean.

In selecting the five churchwardens to initiate the Order of St Iltut, Tom Birt tried to choose them from contrasting parishes. One was from a remote village; another from a suburb; the third from a church in the centre of an industrial town in the north-west of Gyrwas; the fourth from a church in the centre of Kimford which attracted many university lecturers, she herself being a lecturer in mathematics; and the fifth was a young man aged only twenty-four, who had just been elected churchwarden of a large village on the edge of Kimford. They started to meet fortnightly on Saturday mornings, visiting one another's homes.

* * * * *

Iltut's childhood ambition was to be a soldier; and as soon as he was old enough, he left his parents to join the forces of the King of Glamorgan in south Wales. Iltut quickly learnt the skills of fighting, and showed such courage and prowess on the battlefield that within a few years the king appointed him as commander of his army.

Iltut was a keen huntsman, and it was on a hunting expedition with some fellow knights that he was converted to Christianity. The group came across a Christian hermit living in the depths of a forest. The other knights treated him like a slave, demanding that he serve them food and drink. Far from protesting or obeying with sullen resentment, the hermit was happy to prepare a meal for them, serving the finest wild fruits and vegetables which the forest produced. Iltut felt both ashamed of his friends' rudeness and profoundly impressed by the hermit's graceful response. So that evening Iltut rode back to the hermit's hut, to ask him the secret of his radiant and serene personality. They spent the rest of the night in earnest conversation; and at dawn Iltut asked the hermit to baptize him.

The village churchwarden confessed, with a mixture of embarrassment and pride, that he was a retired brigadier, and then added that a surprisingly high proportion of churchwardens are military men. The university mathematician asked if, in his opinion, military service was a good preparation for being a churchwarden. After a long pause, as if the question had never occurred to him before, the brigadier replied, 'My answer must be a diplomatic rather than a military one – yes and no. The soldier's obsession with order is good: the church affairs should be properly ordered. But the church is a voluntary organization, so it's no good barking out orders and expecting people to leap to attention. I've had to learn to hold my tongue.'

The suburban churchwarden, who earned his living as an accountant, agreed, saying that he had had to learn the opposite lesson. 'When I first became a churchwarden, I thought I could be relaxed and sloppy. I have to be so tight and precise at work, that I wanted to go easy in the church. So I let things slide a bit. I didn't bother to send out minutes and agendas in advance of meetings. A couple of times we ran out of wine for communion, and the service was delayed while someone ran to buy some more. I forgot to arrange for the builder to repair a leak, so when a thunderstorm broke out during a service the people in the pews below got wet. In the nicest possible way, people told me to pull my socks up. One woman told me that she could only concentrate on worship if she knew that things were under control. So I'm now quite military in my approach.'

'So how do you get people to do things?' the young churchwarden asked. He said that he had felt immensely flattered to be elected churchwarden, but now wondered if the people were really voting themselves an easy time; his youthful energy ensured that he could do most of the administrative chores himself, but he lacked the authority to persuade others to help him. The churchwarden from the industrial town, an elderly woman who used to run a factory canteen, said that a direct request to an individual is the Christian equivalent of a military command. 'It's no good asking for volunteers; people never put themselves forward. You must go up to people, and ask them to do such-and-such – be quite precise about what you want. They rarely say no.' 'That sounds like moral pressure to me,' said the young man. 'So what?' she answered. 'You're quite right,' the brigadier said to her, 'but I find it terribly difficult to do. I feel as though I am begging for help.' 'That's precisely what you are doing,' she replied.

* * * * *

Iltut never returned to the King's castle, but went to the coast of Glamorgan, and built himself a hut near a sandy beach. He spent the next three months teaching himself how to pray. Meanwhile the King was sending out soldiers to search for Iltut; and when at last some soldiers found him, and told the King what he was doing, the King immediately rode out to talk to Iltut himself. When the King arrived he was furious, accusing Iltut of betraying him. But just as the hermit's grace had melted Iltut's heart, now Iltut's grace melted the King's heart. The King knelt down and begged forgiveness for his anger. Iltut lifted him up and embraced him warmly. Then the King asked Iltut if he would take his eldest son, and educate him.

Over the following twenty years the land behind the beach became the site of a vast college, in which young men from all over Britain and Ireland came to learn both academic subjects and practical skills. Amongst Iltut's pupils were David, who went on to found Wales's greatest monastery and became her patron saint; and Samson, who reformed the monastery on Caldey Island, and then crossed the sea to Brittany, where he preached the gospel with great success. Iltut himself had a particular interest in agriculture, pioneering a new method of ploughing which he persuaded many local farmers to adopt.

The college soon grew too big for Iltut to manage on his own, so he gathered round him a team of people to share the task of management. When they met to make decisions, he encouraged vigorous debate, but also insisted that they should listen to one another without interrupting. He taught them that it was a sign of moral strength, not of weakness, to change one's mind in the light of what others say, and that through listening to one another carefully they would eventually hear the voice of the Holy Spirit.

'If only our parochial church council meetings could be like that,' the mathematician sighed. 'They all seem to think they're so clever – and they love the sound of their own voices.' 'Our problem's just the opposite,' the retired canteen manager said. 'They want the vicar and me to do all the talking – they just want to be led.' The young man added, 'It's no good asking people to listen to each other if they aren't prepared to speak.' So the group began to discuss how they as churchwardens could encourage people both to speak and to listen. The canteen manager wondered if she herself might partly be to blame for wanting to fill the silences. 'If the vicar and I just kept our mouths shut, the other people would be forced to speak.' The mathematician suggested that articulate people, who can easily put their thoughts into words, tend to silence and even drive out the inarticulate. 'In our church council there are two people who never talk at all. And quite a lot of people won't join the council because they don't feel they can stand up to all those fluent dons. They say it's just a talking-shop.'

The young man recalled the first church council he had attended eighteen months previously. The council had been having a quite heated discussion about the prices to charge for refreshments at the summer fête: some wanted high prices to raise more money for the church fabric; others wanted to charge low prices as a gesture of hospitality. The council was evenly divided, and neither side seemed willing to compromise. So the young man suggested that they all spend two minutes in silent prayer, asking for the Spirit's guidance. There was an awkward pause. Then an old farmer exclaimed: 'If we bring the Holy Spirit in, we'll be here all bloody night.' So the discussion carried on without prayer – and continued for a further twenty minutes.

The rest of the group congratulated him on his courage, but suggested that pride had prevented the council from accepting such a wise suggestion from their most youthful member. 'Yes, I may have seemed a bit sanctimonious,' the young man said, 'but isn't prayer – or rather the lack of it – at the heart of what we're saying?' He suggested that people do not listen to each other because they are not in the frame of mind to listen to God. And equally the silent ones do not speak because they are not expecting their thoughts and words to be guided by God. 'Perhaps our council meetings would work better if they were more like prayer meetings – and it's our job as churchwardens to ensure that they are like that,' the young man concluded.

'But isn't that the vicar's job?' the brigadier said. 'He's in charge of the spiritual side of things.' The accountant reminded the brigadier that Bishop Tom Birt had specifically spoken of administration as a spiritual ministry; thus it is the churchwarden's job to ensure that the administrative side of the church's affairs is conducted in a spiritual fashion. This led the group to consider whether churchwardens should chair church council meetings. The brigadier was initially hostile to this idea: 'The vicar is the boss, so he should be in charge of meetings.' 'Or she,' said the mathematician. 'Or not,' said the accountant, 'because under the Celtic way of doing things, we don't have a boss any more. The ordained clergy are pastors or preachers, so it's ridiculous to imagine they can chair meetings. In fact, most of them can't.' 'Nor can many churchwardens,' replied the brigadier. 'In which case they shouldn't be churchwardens,' said the accountant.

'The point is,' said the mathematician, 'that no one is very sure what the churchwarden's job is. I spend a lot of my time plugging gaps, doing jobs which the vicar or somebody else should have done. We're glorified dogsbodies. But if it were clear that we are the managers of the church, overseeing its material affairs and co-ordinating its various activities, then we'd know where we stood. And the congregation would elect people suited to that task.'

*   *   *   *   *

Eventually Iltut grew weary of his busy life; and he felt that the time had come for a new leader to take over the college he had founded, with fresh zeal and vision. So he announced that he would step down the following Easter. Everyone was appalled, and begged him to remain in charge. After much persuasion he relented, promising to remain in office for an extra year. The months passed, and Iltut made no further mention of retirement, so people hoped that he had put the idea out of his mind. Then on the night of Easter, when everyone had fallen asleep after the celebrations, Iltut slipped out of the college grounds. He spent the remainder of his life as a hermit on the Gower peninsula. In due course a successor was appointed who proved extremely capable, and the college continued to flourish.

'None of us is indispensable,' said the mathematician, 'and I certainly don't want to go on indefinitely. Five years is my limit, then I'll let someone else take over.' 'That's all very well for you in the city, in a church chock-full of able people,' responded the brigadier, 'but in my tiny parish there's no one else willing to do the job, let alone up to it. After all, we're lucky to get half a dozen in church on Sunday mornings, and three of those are over 80.' 'I don't want to seem heartless,' said the accountant, 'but what happens when you're past it?' 'God only knows,' the brigadier replied.

'Yes, God does know,' the young man interjected. 'It's not up to us how long we serve as churchwardens – it's up to God.' 'So how do I know when to stop?' asked the canteen manager. 'You pray about it,' replied the young man. 'And you listen to what the congregation may think and feel,' added the accountant. 'As we said earlier, God can speak through anyone and everyone. After all, it is the congregation who elects us.' 'And when has a congregation ever dismissed a churchwarden?' asked the canteen manager. 'We mustn't expect them to dismiss us,' replied the accountant. 'Like Iltut, we must discern the signs – picking up critical remarks, sensing that we are stifling new ideas, and so on. And the clearest sign is that there is a good replacement.'

* * * * *

In February 2006 Tom Birt came to see the five churchwardens. He wished to write to all the parishes in Gyrwas Diocese, reminding them that the men and women they elected as churchwardens at the spring-time annual general meetings would shortly afterwards become members of the Order of St Iltut. Tom Birt wanted the five founding members to enclose a letter with his, outlining the ministry of churchwardens as they now understood it, and describing the qualities and abilities which a churchwarden should possess.

In trying to answer these questions, which appeared straightforward enough, the group found itself saying that they were the wrong questions to ask. In theory the ministry of churchwardens is, and always has been, clear: managing the parish. The real questions are: How should the task of management be conducted within a Christian institution? And how does this ministry relate to the other ministries in the church? The group then reported to Tom Birt their thoughts about the need to combine efficiency with gentleness, and the challenge of infusing council meetings with a spirit of prayer. Tom Birt asked how churchwardens could acquire those skills of Christian management. 'The way the managers of business acquire them,' answered the accountant. 'They go on courses.' The mathematician told of the management course on which she had been sent after her appointment as head of department: 'It was just common sense, dressed up in diagrams.' 'The trouble with common sense,' the accountant replied, 'is that we easily ignore it. Over these past few months of meeting one another, we've been re-learning common sense – with the help of Iltut and the Bible. All I'm saying is that other churchwardens might benefit in the same way.'

Tom Birt nudged the discussion to the second question. 'Despite my initial reservations,' the brigadier said, 'I've been persuaded that most clergy do too much administration – and tend to do it badly. They would be delighted to leave it to the specialists.' Tom Birt replied that, since most clergy had now been affirmed as either pastors or preachers, they should be relinquishing their administrative tasks. The accountant said that, as far as he could observe, that was not happening. 'Since many of the clergy are still paid salaries, and everyone else is voluntary, the lay people still expect the clergy to manage the church.' Tom Birt asked how this situation could be altered. 'We feel that the key,' the accountant said, 'is for churchwardens to take over the church councils. In almost all organizations, especially voluntary ones, the person chairing the meetings is also the senior manager – and is seen to be.'

'If churchwardens become chairmen,' said the mathematician, 'I don't think you need spell out their ministry, because it will be obvious. Nor will you need to stipulate the qualities needed in churchwardens; the people on the ground can judge who is likely to chair meetings well.' So instead of writing to parishes, Tom Birt wrote to members of the Order of St Cuthbert, asking them if, at the forthcoming annual general meeting, they would nominate the church-wardens formally as deputy chairmen, indicating that in future a churchwarden would take the chair at council meetings. In the meantime, the founding members of the Order of St Iltut began to plan courses for churchwardens in the art of Christian management.

EPILOGUE

The Order of St Brendan

By the middle of 2006 all the six Orders were functioning, and roughly a quarter of the regular churchgoers in Gyrwas Diocese belonged to at least one.

The Order of St Aidan, which had started first, had transformed the lives of the two bishops and three archdeacons, and also the image which people had of them. They attended virtually no committee meetings, and spent most of their time visiting parishes. Thus they were no longer seen as remote, awesome figures, but as friendly guides. And people no longer made a distinction in their minds between Tom Birt and the others, regarding them as equals.

The formation of the Order of St Cuthbert caused only modest changes. Almost all the larger parishes in the towns and major villages were able to raise sufficient funds to pay for a full-time pastor. Even those who rarely attended church services proved willing to give generously to retain a pastor in their midst – once they were assured that the money would all go directly for this purpose. Many of the small rural parishes, however, decided that they could not raise enough money to maintain the present number of full-time pastors, so they decided to form larger groups, some with as many as fifteen or twenty parishes. But, to the surprise of many of the clergy and the parishioners, this proved quite workable. Since the Celtic revolution freed the pastors both from administrative duties and from preaching – and since the combined populations of twenty villages may be no more than a town parish – the parishioners received the same level of pastoral care as before. No rural clergy were forced to resign from full-time pastoral work. A few retired. Several decided they wanted only a small group of parishes, or only one, and with the agreement of the parishioners worked only half-time or in their spare time, taking secular employment to compensate. And several more, along with several urban clergy, decided they were called to be exclusively preachers.

Just over a third of those clergy who became full-time pastors decided that they were also called to be preachers, and were accepted as members of the Order of St Patrick. Of those clergy who decided that they were not pastors, and wanted to devote themselves entirely to preaching, only a handful were supported with full salaries by their churches. The others became freelance preachers, receiving fees for each engagement; in every case they had to supplement this income with secular work. About half the Readers in Gyrwas Diocese sought and received membership of the Order; about a quarter were rejected, and the rest decided to retire from preaching. As the years passed, an increasing number of people put themselves forward for training as preachers. Many had felt called for a long time to the ordained ministry, but did not wish to become traditional vicars. Now they realized that their vocation was only to preaching, and the Order of St Patrick provided the context in which they could fulfil themselves.

The Order of St Brigid at first remained very small. The clergy who had become full-time pastors took a few years to adjust to their new situation, and so paid little attention to the healing ministry. But gradually many of them realized that their own ministry could be wonderfully complemented by having a group of healers in the parishes. Pastors with five or ten thousand, or even more, in their parishes, could not hope to visit all who were sick, let alone those suffering other forms of distress. But a team of healers, each covering a specific area, could both hear about people's needs and respond. A growing number of pastors urged members of their congregations with a healing gift to join the Order of St Brigid, as a means of affirming and authorizing their ministry. So the Order steadily expanded.

In addition to organists and choirmasters, a small number of singers, who accompanied themselves by guitar, joined the Order of St Columba. They offered to teach congregations new songs, or to lead the singing in small churches which had no organ. The small churches responded most enthusiastically, inviting them to play at special events, such as Harvest Thanksgivings and Carol Services. Soon the demand for these singer-guitarists was so great that the Order had to advertise in local papers for more. Just over a dozen of the architects who looked after churches in Gyrwas Diocese joined the Order, meeting regularly to discuss ways in which the present generation should make its mark. They then began encouraging the more active parishes to consider new schemes. The most popular proved to be wall-paintings, with a particular interest in depicting gospel stories in the context of the parish itself. Some parishes employed professional artists, but a growing number recruited amateur artists within their own communities.

The main activity of the Order of St Iltut was to run training courses for churchwardens. These courses both increased the confidence of the churchwardens, and raised their status in people's eyes. Thus within a few years almost all the church councils in Gyrwas Diocese had a church-warden as chairman. And this in turn meant that pastors – the parish clergy – were set free of administrative duties.

Across Gyrwas Diocese, ten parishes which manifestly required a full-time pastor, were unable to support one financially. Seven of these were in large estates, built by local governments in the 1960s and '70s. The populations were mainly poor, and only a tiny fraction attended church services or showed any interest in the Church. The other three were in newer estates built by private developers in the previous twenty years. Although the people were richer, the sense of community on these estates was very weak; so again, few were interested in the churches which Gyrwas Diocese had built there. Tom Birt wrote a letter to every parish in Gyrwas Diocese, asking them to support pastors in these places. Instead of administering these funds himself, he would put parishes willing to contribute in touch with the churches in need, so that there would be a direct relationship. Many of the richer parishes in Gyrwas Diocese, aware of their own privilege, proved eager to give.

Tom Birt had expected that the Celtic revolution would

stimulate congregations to grow, since the various Orders between them would reach out to far more people than the traditional vicar. In fact the normal Sunday attendance continued its slow decline. But attendance at the major festivals and special services grew sharply, since more people were engaged in the preparations for them – and because the quality of preaching and of music improved. And, even more significantly, people began to organize services at other times and in other places. Within many parishes or groups of parishes members of the Order of St Brigid met in one another's homes to pray for the sick; evening meetings took place at which members of the Order of St Patrick were invited to speak, allowing them to explore subjects in greater depth than a sermon allows; and pastors held evening Communion services, which attracted those who preferred to sleep late or to go out on Sundays.

* * * * *

In 2007 two Methodist ministers from Kimford went to see Tom Birt, and asked whether they could join the Order of St Patrick. They gave two reasons for this request. The first, they said, was a matter of principle: that Methodism had begun not as a separate denomination, but as a movement within the Church of England whose primary purpose was to improve the quality of preaching; thus, by belonging to the Order of St Patrick, they would be returning to the roots of Methodism. The second was practical: they wished to be allowed to preach in Anglican churches, and also to invite Anglican preachers regularly into their own pulpits.

Tom Birt replied that his initial reaction was wholly favourable, but they were raising issues that went far beyond their own request. The response would thus require two steps. Firstly, the diocesan synod would have to decide in principle whether members of other denominations should be allowed to join the six Orders. Secondly, each Order would have to determine its procedure for admitting them, since to a great extent the individual Orders were responsible for their own affairs.

The first step was led by one of the archdeacons, who made an eloquent speech at the next synod, arguing that the Orders could become a powerful force for unity between the Christian denominations. The Celtic tradition is common to all churches in the British Isles; and as a symbol of this he referred to the two great cathedrals in Armagh, one Anglican and the other Roman Catholic, both dedicated to St Patrick. The six Orders which Gyrwas Diocese now had, based on the Celtic model of ministry, were primarily fellowships of people with the same vocation, providing mutual support and encouragement. Since these vocations are not confined to the Church of England, but are equally present in every denomination, the Orders should be extended to include every denomination. 'Indeed,' the archdeacon concluded, 'Anglicans will surely be enriched in their various ministries by the insights and experiences of other churches.'

The second speaker, a vicar in an ecumenical project on the edge of Kimford, said the Anglicans were often criticized by members of other denominations for wanting Christian unity on their own terms; and he feared that extending the six Orders, as the archdeacon proposed, could be seen as another example of this. It was, therefore, important that Anglican rules should not be imposed on members of other denominations; instead they should be accepted in the Orders according to their own rules.

The third speaker, a solicitor from a rural parish, said that this could prove highly problematic, since the Church of England is bound by complex canon laws which could not be bent. 'A Methodist minister could not, for example, become the pastor of an Anglican parish church without first leaving the Methodist Church and joining the Church of England – and then seeking ordination. Nor could the minister of another denomination regularly preach in Anglican churches without going through the same process. And what sense does it make to have an Order exclusively for churchwardens if this exclusivity is instantly breached?' He asserted that he favoured Christian unity in theory, but wished to draw the synod's attention to the practical problems.

The vicar from the ecumenical project rose again to suggest that the entire diocese be turned into a vast ecumenical project, in which the different denominations formally recognized and authorized one another's clergy. The archdeacon replied that such a proposal was premature – it was the end of the process that the synod was considering, not the beginning. His idea was that people from other denominations could join the six Orders on the basis of Christian fellowship, and this would provide a context in which closer bonds of unity would gradually be forged. In answer to the solicitor, he said that there would be no need to infringe canon law: the clergy of each denomination would continue to conduct services and to preach primarily within their own churches. With that reassurance the archdeacon's motion was passed with a large majority.

The second step was made remarkably quickly. The bishops and archdeacons invited those in equivalent positions in other churches to start attending meetings of the Order of St Aidan, to discuss how they could co-operate more closely. The Methodist chairman of the district, the Baptist superintendent, the United Reformed Church moderator and the Roman Catholic bishop all accepted. The Order of St Cuthbert invited ministers, priests and elders from other churches, who saw themselves primarily as pastors, to join them, with the intention of giving one another spiritual and moral support. About half of those invited accepted. The Order of St Patrick was unwilling to drop its procedure for vetting preachers, since this would undermine the purpose of the Order. None the less a number of priests, ministers and local preachers asked to join, wishing to have their preaching ministry re-affirmed and supported. The Order of St Iltut decided to invite all those in charge of administration in their churches to join; their only stipulation was that members should not be ordained clergy. The Orders of St Brigid and St Columba decided that denominational loyalty was irrelevant to their respective ministries, and extended an open invitation.

The consequences of this process over the following decade were enormous; yet they seemed so natural and easy, that people hardly remarked upon them. When the bishops and archdeacons visited Anglican parishes, they often visited other churches in their localities; and equally moderators and chairmen went to Anglican churches during their tours. Since the bishops no longer wore special clothes, people around Gyrwas became increasingly uncertain of – and indifferent to – the distinction between these various types of leader. Some called all of them 'bishops'; others referred to them as 'elders'.

Initially in rural areas where ordained clergy were most scarce, and then increasingly in towns, churches of different denominations decided to share pastors. In some cases the motive was financial, since more congregations could share the burden of raising the pastor's salary. But the main stimulus was from the pastors themselves. The Order of St Cuthbert quickly formed local branches, with members meeting each month. At first they simply discussed their work, talking about the challenges and problems they each found. Then some branches began to co-ordinate their weekday activities, with different pastors specializing in the kind of visiting and counselling that suited their gifts and temperaments. Finally they co-ordinated their worship. On Sundays they held fewer services in each church, encouraging congregations to visit one another's services. And the growing number of midweek services in people's homes were organized jointly. Once this stage had been reached, most branches of the Order asked their churches whether they could be paid as a team; and since their congregations now saw them in this light, they happily responded.

This in turn forced a similar process to occur within the Order of St Patrick. The men and women invited to preach at joint services generally belonged to the denomination in whose church the service was taking place. But since the congregations naturally wanted a high standard of preaching, it was agreed in most places that preachers in all the churches should belong to the Order of St Patrick. This meant that priests, ministers and local preachers of every denomination, if they wished to continue preaching, had no choice but to apply for membership of the Order.

As pastorship and preaching became ecumenical in many areas, so the other three Orders quickly followed. Those in charge of administration of the churches formed joint councils. Singers and musicians moved freely between churches as they were invited. And the pastoral teams worked together in nurturing and affirming the healing ministry.

Thus by a process of spiritual evolution at local level, rather than by legal resolution from above, the vision of the vicar on the edge of Kimford was largely realized: most of Gyrwas became an ecumenical project. By the year 2012 the members of the Order of St Aidan were wondering whether to conduct joint ordination of preachers and pastors, thus completing the merger of the different denominations, and they decided to seek legal advice as to how this could be done.

*   *   *   *   *

When Tom Birt had begun forming orders of ministry, he had imagined himself sparking a revolution, which would first transform Gyrwas Diocese, and then spread outwards across the land. For the sake of his own soul he had made some attempts to quell such thoughts, for fear of becoming boastful. He need not have worried. Indeed his knowledge of church history should have taught him better. As he found himself reflecting around the year 2013, the Church of England has over the centuries proved adept at taming her revolutions, turning them into gentle movements. And that was the fate of Tom Birt's activities.

Bishops, clergy and laity in other dioceses, especially those like Gyrwas facing acute financial problems, looked on with interest. At first there was more hostility and suspicion outside Gyrwas than there was within, as Tom Birt's vision was seen as an assault on the authority of the ordained priesthood. Some dismissed Tom Birt as an enthusiastic newcomer, who would soon be defeated by the entrenched interests and solid traditions of the Church of England. But once the clergy of Gyrwas were playing leading roles in the new orders, opposition quietened. And most observers recognized that the success of Tom Birt's scheme lay in its fidelity to tradition: it went with, not against, the grain of Anglican history.

The General Synod, meeting for its winter session in London, held a brief debate on events in Gyrwas, as the basis of a motion proposing that the same six orders of ministry be instituted throughout the Church of England. The motion was rejected in favour of an amendment, stating that dioceses should be free to institute new orders of ministry according to their needs and circumstances.

By 2013 three other dioceses had begun copying Gyrwas's scheme in its entirety, while five more were instituting some new orders of ministry on Tom Birt's lines. Elsewhere the initiative was being taken by groups of clergy and laity, without formal approval. Priests and Readers keen to promote better preaching were forming local Orders of St Patrick. In some places archdeacons and rural deans were encouraging churchwardens in each deanery to form an Order of St Iltut. And in many parishes and areas people concerned with the healing ministry were meeting for prayer and mutual support, often under the banner of St Brigid. Artists, who are usually quite individualistic in temperament, and also more diverse in their activities, were less ready to form groups. And many parish clergy, where there was no financial threat to their jobs, saw little point in forming a new order, when they already met other clergy regularly at local chapters.

Tom Birt thought of the peculiar fate of the Tractarian Movement in the nineteenth century, which aroused great controversy by promoting a return to more catholic styles of ministry and worship. After thirty or forty years most of its ideas were regarded as common sense, and no longer seen as particularly catholic – in fact they were espoused by many who believed themselves to be staunch Protestants. Tom Birt foresaw a time when the Celtic approach to ministry would be taken for granted in the Church of England – not necessarily in the precise form in which he formulated it, but in a variety of different ways. Then his pioneering efforts in Gyrwas would be almost entirely forgotten.

* * * * *

By 2015 Tom Birt had served as Bishop of Gyrwas for fifteen years, and had grown old in the job. A warning uttered by John Chrysostom, a bishop of the early Church, echoed in his mind: that bishops will find it especially difficult to enter the Kingdom of Heaven, because their job induces the deepest of all sins, spiritual pride. He was now revered throughout Gyrwas, Britain and beyond as a great visionary and pioneer, and also as a humble and prayerful man; but he recognized that this reverence undermined the virtue of humility. He thus announced that he would retire at Christmas of that year; and he and his wife began to wonder where they would live for their remaining years on earth.

A few days after this announcement an elderly woman rang the bell of his house. His secretary answered the door. The woman said that she was an old acquaintance of Tom Birt from his days as a vicar in Gyrwas Diocese. The secretary ushered her into the waiting room; and twenty minutes later, when Tom Birt had a gap in his schedule of appointments, the secretary took her into his study.

At first Tom Birt did not recognize her. 'I am Peggy,' she said, 'that awkward, argumentative woman that used to come to your services.' The Bishop remembered her well. 'Where have you been all these years?' he asked. 'Still in the parish where you were vicar,' she replied. 'But I've kept out of your way, because I didn't want to embarrass you.' He paused, wondering what she meant; then he blushed. 'Yes,' he said, 'I've often thought of you over these years. When I thought of the Celtic scheme for Gyrwas, I assumed it was my idea; and that's what everyone believed. But then a few months later I realized that it was you who had suggested it fifteen years earlier, in a conversation in my vicarage study. I wasn't a bishop then, so it seemed irrelevant – and a bit barmy. Still, I should have given you credit.' 'No you shouldn't,' she answered, 'and I didn't want you to. It would have made you seem stupid. That's why I've kept a low profile.'

There was a long silence. Then Peggy said, 'I've come to tell you that you've left out one of the ancient Celtic Orders.' 'Which one is that?' asked Tom Birt. 'Pilgrims,' she replied, 'the people who wandered wherever the Spirit led. Their patron is Brendan, who set sail from the west of Ireland, and went wherever the wind took him – even as far as America.' 'Did you mention pilgrims when you told me your ideas thirty years ago?' Tom Birt asked. 'No I didn't, because the world today has too little space for that kind of pilgrim; roads and aeroplanes go everywhere. Besides, we need another kind of pilgrim today: pilgrims of the soul, who wander into uncharted spiritual places.'

Tom Birt asked what she meant. 'Well, there are two ways in which Christians can be pilgrims. First, there is the journey of living out our faith in our lives, in all their joys and sorrows. Being a pilgrim in faith is not easy, but we have to keep on keeping on because we are following in the footsteps of the disciples, the original pilgrims. Then secondly, we have to witness to that faith to everyone around us, those we already know and those we don't. In the past few years you have wandered outside the boundaries of the Church of England into the territory of other denominations, and as a result you've continued the journey towards Christian unity. But those routes are well charted – people have been exploring Christian unity for over a century. And what's more, there has been little opposition, since nearly all Christians believe that unity between them is desirable, even if they often quarrel about how to achieve it.

'But there is another, rather more perilous, journey to make, where the maps are sketchier, and that is the search for at least some degree of unity between faith communities throughout the world. That route goes beyond the boundaries of Christianity, sometimes into the territory of the other religions, and then opposition can be strong.'

'And who do you suggest makes that journey?' asked Tom Birt. 'You,' Peggy replied, 'because it follows on from the journey you've already made by embracing Celtic Christianity. Our Celtic ancestors did not see the natural world as matter without spirit, but they saw the light of God in every human being, and every animal and bird, insect and plant. So if we follow their path we should expect to find some of Christ's light shining in everything, including all the great religions of the world. And if we first try to establish some spiritual unity across the world, then we may be able to nurture that practical political unity which may save this world from destruction.'

'It is a huge task – too big for an old bishop on the point of retirement,' was his response. 'Discovering America,' she replied, 'was a huge task for a young monk, but Brendan managed it.' 'All right,' said the bishop. 'But Brendan had companions on his journey. Who will accompany me?' 'Yes, you must have companions,' said Peggy, 'otherwise you will lose heart. Your first companion must be your wife; you should only undertake this journey if she will come with you. And my husband and I will also come – in fact we've started already.'

'Another question,' said Tom Birt. 'Brendan and his friends rowed from time to time to get them to America. What must we do to explore the spiritual world?' 'The only thing we can do, which is to pray,' replied Peggy. 'Christians have always been happy to explore the spiritual world of the Jews, by singing their psalms and reading their scriptures. We could sing the psalms and read the scriptures of other faiths as well.'

'One last question. Brendan and his friends lived in a coracle. Where are we to live?' 'If you and your wife are happy to have us as companions,' answered Peggy, 'come and live in our village – where you were vicar, years ago. And you can join us every morning in the church – to pray with the world.'

Which is just what Tom Birt and his wife did.